CRIME AND CORRECTIONS

CRIME and CORRECTIONS

Lessons Learned by a Career Corrections Practitioner

THOMAS TOOMBS, PhD

LUMINARE PRESS

To Ed Ben

WWII Veteran—Siletz Tribal Elder

Unsung Hero in Oregon State Penitentiary Riot,
March 1968

(See Appendix)

Table of Contents

LESSON 4:
Efforts to Reform Prisons Should Be Abandoned in Favor of Efforts to Develop High-Tech Alternatives

Preface

I was 22 years old and I had no intention of making a career working in corrections. Circumstances and unexpected events, however, led to a lengthy career. I spent more than 30 years as a corrections practitioner, operating prisons and correctional institutions, administering programs for adult criminals, juvenile offenders, and the criminally insane, including a stint as the head of Oregon's adult corrections system.

Throughout my career there was an ever present aura of tension and uncertainty in the workplace that was a by-product of the ongoing disagreement between those who promote a "get tough" approach to crime, and those who argue for a "less punitive" approach. This dichotomy is referred to as "punishment versus treatment."

Many have characterized this dichotomy as being analogous to the motion of a pendulum swinging back and forth between two extremes. I always thought the dichotomy was more analogous to a mobile. The path of a pendulum, its speed, and moment it will change direction are all measurable and predictable. In contrast, a mobile swirls, darts, bobs, and skips—unpredictably changing direction in response to the whims of the wind.

Correctional policy and practice, past and present, is created in much the same way a mobile moves; driven by the winds of myth, intuition, and ignorance generated by uninformed or uneducated politicians, practitioners, academicians, judges and select others exercising the prerogatives of power they hold.

This book is intended to serve legislators, practitioners, academicians, and students of criminal justice. My goal is to pass along to others involved in criminal justice related employment or academic studies lessons learned during my career with the hope these lessons will:

- Persuade policy makers, practitioners, academicians and students that contrary to popular belief the cause of criminal behavior is unknown and neither punishment nor rehabilitation effectively deter or prevent criminal behavior;

- Encourage them to redirect some effort and resources into scientific research designed to determine what causes criminal behavior, and

- Urge them to stop trying to reform prisons and develop alternatives for prisons using advanced technology

Foreword

I have known the author professionally for over forty years. For most of these years I have been privileged to consider him not just a colleague but my friend. Both he and I spent more than thirty years as correctional professionals.

When I began my corrections career, the author was the Deputy Administrator for the Oregon Corrections Division. I was working as a correctional officer in the Oregon Women's Correctional Center (OWCC). I promoted through the security ranks and completed a graduate program (Master's degree) in Correctional Administration at Western Oregon University.

Shortly after the author became the Administrator of Oregon Corrections Division in 1985, I was promoted to Assistant Superintendent at OWCC. This was my first opportunity to work more closely with the author and benefit from his leadership style, which is based on the principles of Action Research developed by Kurt Lewin considered the founder of modern day Social Psychology. The author consistently challenged me to fully participate in policy discussions, share my ideas and eventually become a better leader myself.   This leadership experience served me especially well when I became superintendent.

My most rewarding professional experience was working with the author as a member of a team tasked with developing a prototype design for new prisons to be constructed by the State of Oregon in the future. More than twenty years after our design team experience, I have come to accept that building more and supposedly better prisons is expensive and does not effectively address the real issues regarding crime and punishment.

This book is worth reading because the author is a credible expert in the criminal justice field. He has worked in all levels of the system, having been a practitioner, administrator, scholar, adjunct professor, researcher and author. The author's reason for writing this book is to persuade and encourage present day as well as future policy makers, practitioners and academicians to abandon old corrections policies and practices and develop new approaches based on more certain knowledge of what causes criminal behavior. He hopes the lessons he learned during his career, discussed in this book, will help others change and improve the corrections system instead of continuing to promote and apply the failed policies and practices of the past.

Since being asked to write the foreword for this book, I have reflected on both the lessons learned by the author as well as what I have learned after more than four decades in corrections. I share the author's belief that corrections is past due for a new approach. I hope for a time when validated scientific research guides systemic change. And, I dream of a time when prisons are demolished and funding used to operate prisons is diverted to build schools and sustain other essential human service programs.

—Sonia E. Hoyt, Retired Superintendent
Oregon Department of Corrections

LESSON 1:
The Cause of Criminal Behavior is Unknown

LESSON 1:
The Cause of Criminal Behavior is Unknown

Theories about what causes criminal behavior have been traced back to Plato in the *Laws* published in circa 348 BC (Smith Prangle 2009). Today there are at least nine categories of theories postulating what causes criminal behavior. No theory has been validated by data collected using the scientific method. It seems pretty obvious that both the cause of and the remedy for criminal behavior are unknown based on the fact that people throughout the world continue to commit crimes no matter what theoretical approach is applied to correct or deter the behavior.

Theories of what causes criminal behavior are divided between two schools of thought: the classical school and the positivist school. The primary difference between the two schools is the foundation upon which the school is grounded.

The cornerstone of the classical school is the belief that criminal behavior is an expression of free will, a voluntary act committed after careful consideration of the consequences. The most effective deterrent/remedy for criminal behavior, according to classical school thinkers, is punishment and the threat thereof.

The guiding premise of the positivist school is that criminal behavior is caused by a circumstance, condition, or factor—a psychological trauma, deprived socioeconomic circumstances, medical condition, or hereditary influence—over which the offender had or has no control. Positivist school theories assert prevention of criminal behavior requires elimination of or compensation for the causative factors.

Classical School Theory

Methods of Punishment:
- Probation
- Incarceration
- Capital Punishment

The concept of punishment and its capacity to alter behavior has been the subject of speculation for centuries by scholars and thinkers such as Cesare Beccaria, Jeremy Bentham, Voltaire, Denis Diderot, David Hume, Adam Smith, Thomas Paine, Immanuel Kant, Georg Wilhelm Hegel, Friedrich Nietzsche, and B. F. Skinner.

Rational choice theory—also known as situational theory or control theory 2—is one of today's more popular examples of classical school thinking. According to this theory, all people are selfishly motivated. Each person identifies his or her wants and desires, prioritizes them, and selects a means of achieving them that offers the greatest probability of success. Poverty, unemployment, broken homes, illiteracy, poor health care, or an injured psyche do not breed criminals, the theory postulates. Criminals use these factors as excuses to justify their behavior (Clarke and Mayhew 1980; Elster 1986; Jeffery 1971; Scott 1999; Laycock 2001).

 THOMAS TOOMBS, PhD

Proponents of rational choice theory argue that if the commission of a crime is made difficult and the penalty is sufficiently harsh, anyone considering a criminal act will rationally decide the effort required to commit the crime is too high, the consequences if caught are too high, or both.

Strategies for effective crime-prevention programs based on rational choice theory require three fundamental elements: 1) discarding the idea that criminal behavior is caused by social, psychological, economic, or biological factors; 2) making it harder for crimes to be committed and easier for criminals to be caught; and 3) ensuring harsh punishment. Proponents of this theory strongly support mandatory prison terms, the elimination of parole, life sentences after a third felony conviction (the so-called "three strikes" rule), and capital punishment.

To make it harder for criminals to commit crimes, rational choice enthusiasts advocate mapping criminal activity and flooding the areas where most crime is committed with police, video surveillance systems, intrusion detection systems, and security patrols. Citizens are encouraged to install security hardware on the doors and windows of their homes and businesses as well as to avail themselves of self-defense and firearms training.

One example of the rational choice approach to crime prevention can be seen in the increasing number of gated residential communities in the United States over the past 20 years. It could be argued that, universally applied, this approach to crime prevention would result in a kind of role reversal: noncriminals would be securely confined in walled, gated, and guarded compounds while criminals would be free to roam the streets at will.

Methods of Punishment

The methods used to punish criminals in the United States are generally limited to probation, incarceration, or capital punishment.

Probation

Probation is a form of sentencing—sometimes confused with parole—imposed by the sentencing judge that allows a convicted criminal to live in the community, subject to conditions ordered by the judge and enforced by a probation officer, who reports to the judge. In some instances, the criminal is required to complete a jail sentence (typically no more than one year) before being released on probation. Failure to satisfactorily complete the conditions of probation may result in the criminal being sentenced to a term in prison.

The term "parolee" is applied to a person who is granted a release from prison by a parole board, not a sentencing judge, and allowed to return to the community (subject to conditions ordered by the parole board and enforced by a parole officer who reports to the parole board). A parole board is a select group of individuals appointed by the governor.

The conditions imposed on probationers and parolees typically include abstaining from alcohol and drugs, avoiding contact or association with other criminals, maintaining gainful employment, and participating in specialized substance abuse, mental health, or sex offender treatment if the person has a mental health issue or history of substance abuse.

Although many people do not consider probation to be punishment, probation is the sanction most frequently used by the courts to punish a criminal offender. According to data collected and analyzed by the US Bureau of Justice Statistics, the number of convicted felons under supervision as probationers in the United States during 2014 was 3,789,785, nearly three times the number of incarcerated felons (1,476,847.) In Oregon, the number of probationers in 2014 was 37,923, and the number of inmates was 15,075. Nationally, a convicted felon is roughly three times more likely to be placed on probation than to go to prison, regardless of their criminal offense, and roughly twice as likely in Oregon.

In 1995, the Bureau of Justice Statistics released a report entitled "Probation and Parole Violators in State Prison, 1991" (Cohen 1995). The purpose of the study was to determine how many inmates committed to prison were on probation or parole when they were incarcerated.

- According to the report, 459,337 criminals were committed to state prisons in 1991, and 162,000 (35 percent) of them had been on probation when they were incarcerated. Seventy-four percent of the 162,000 had been convicted of committing a new crime. The remaining 26 percent had their probation revoked by the court for violating one or more of the conditions of their probation.

- The average amount of time criminals spent on probation before committing a violation was 17 months. During the 17-month period, those violators committed 44,000 violent crimes, 3,500 property crimes, and 30,000 drug-related crimes.

Incarceration

Criminals are incarcerated in either a jail or prison. Jails are normally operated by local government and are used to confine a suspected criminal pending the outcome of their trial or for a short period—one year or less—after conviction. Prisons, normally operated by state governments or the federal government, are used to confine criminals for sentences that exceed one year.

America is criticized at home and abroad for its incarceration rate: 716 per 100,000, which is ranked as the highest in the world. In terms of total numbers, other nations have more people incarcerated (for example, China has more than 9 million incarcerated). According to the Bureau of Justice Statistics, 1,476, 847 convicted felons were confined in federal and state prisons in 2014; 15,075 were incarcerated in Oregon's prisons. Jails in the United States held an average daily population of 721,300.

Many people have a misconception of what life inside a prison is like. Some believe prisons are like hotels or spas in which prisoners are allowed to lounge around and sunbathe every day, weather permitting.

In reality, prison is not a leisurely experience. In prison, someone in authority makes almost every decision for a prisoner. Someone other than the prisoner determines the sleep schedule, what clothing can be worn, when to shower, when and what to eat, when and where to work, who may visit, when and where they may visit, how long a visit can last, and how frequently visits may occur.

Prisoners prepare and serve all meals. They clean, sweep, and dust the institution to keep it free of lice, mice, and other vermin.

Inmates wash all the clothing and bed covers. They

 THOMAS TOOMBS, PhD

paint and repair facilities and equipment, including the plumbing and heating systems. Landscape crews mow and maintain the lawns and prune the shrubbery and trees. Prisoners are assigned to work in the infirmary and industry programs such as furniture making. Like any city, in the broader community there are not enough jobs to put every inmate to work.

Meals for the general population are typically served cafeteria-style three times daily in a large dining room (not unlike a school cafeteria, except that the tables and stools are bolted to the floor). Depending on the size of the prison, it may take up to three hours to serve a meal to the entire population, and each inmate may be allowed no more than 15 minutes to eat.

The concept of privacy is just a memory for prisoners. Prisoners typically bathe in group showers similar to school locker rooms. Clothing is centrally laundered and exchanged once per week unless a prisoner has a job that requires more frequent clothing exchange. Toilets have no privacy screens and are open to facilitate observation and security supervision.

Most of the prison population goes about its daily schedule (work, school, recreation, and medical appointments) without incident. A percentage of the inmates, however, continue to engage in criminal activity; stealing, robbing, assaulting, raping, or even murdering other prisoners or staff, just as they did on the outside.

To prevent weaker prisoners from being abused, harassed, assaulted, compelled to pay for protection, or share their private property with more aggressive prisoners, the architecture and operation of prisons are designed to ensure that no one prisoner has influence or control over another.

Prison rules and operating procedures are, by design, intended to promote uniformity and prevent one inmate from influencing the behavior of or having control over the activity of another inmate.

Prisoners who break institutional rules or commit crimes are confined to the prison jail, commonly called a segregation unit. Depending on how dangerous he or she is, the prisoner may be allowed out of the cell for no more than one hour per day to shower and exercise. If the prisoner poses a serious threat to others, he or she may be placed in leg irons and shackles before the cell door is opened.

Prisons are generally classified as one of four types: super maximum security, maximum security, medium security, or minimum security. Many corrections systems also operate camps and halfway houses, also called transitional living centers. Starting with the most secure type of facility (super maximum) and descending to the least secure (halfway houses), each facility is designed, constructed, and operated to maintain control over the prisoners by restricting their ability to move freely inside the facility and making it increasingly more difficult to escape.

1. Super Maximum Security Prisons
    Super maximum security prisons are designed to house prisoners who have a long, established history of violent behavior, who pose a severe threat to the physical well-being of other inmates and prison personnel, and who would also pose a severe threat to the general public if they escaped.

    Inmates are confined to a single-occupancy cell for 23 hours a day. They are allowed out of the cell for one hour each day to exercise and shower, during which time they may be placed in handcuffs connected to a belly chain and leg irons, depending on the physical threat they pose to others.

2. Maximum Security Prisons

Maximum security prisons house prisoners who have exhibited aggressive behavior but have not established a pattern of violent behavior while in confinement. They are considered less of a threat to the health and well-being of other inmates, prison personnel, and the general public.

Inmates are permitted to engage in group activities and allowed out of their cells each day to eat, work, exercise, shower, participate in self-improvement programs, attend religious services if they choose, and receive visits.

3. Medium Security Prisons

Medium security prisons house inmates who have minimal or no history of violent or aggressive behavior and are considered a moderate threat to the health and well-being of other inmates, prison personnel, and the general public.

Accommodations in a medium security prison may include a mixture of single-occupancy cells, multiple-occupancy cells, and multiple-occupancy dormitories. Dormitories resemble military barracks and are equipped with bunk beds stacked two high, footlockers for storing clothing and personal property, group toilets, a shower area, and sinks.

Inmates are allowed out of their quarters every day to eat, work, exercise, shower, participate in self-improvement programs, attend religious services if they choose, and receive visits.

4. Minimum Security Prisons
Minimum security prisons house inmates who present no apparent threat to the life, health, or safety of other inmates or prison personnel and are not considered an escape risk or a threat to the general public if they escaped.

The perimeter of a minimum security prison typically does not have a security fence; if it does, a single fence is normally used. Unarmed guards conduct random patrols inside and outside the building(s). There are no watchtowers.

Accommodations are typically multiple-occupancy dormitories or oversized rooms. These facilities often resemble military barracks and are equipped with bunk beds, sometimes stacked two high, lockers for storage of clothing and personal property, enough toilets and sinks to serve the occupants (though not on an individual basis), and group shower facilities like those found in public school gyms.

Inmates are allowed out of their living quarters each day to eat, work, exercise, shower, participate in self-improvement programs, attend religious services if they choose, and receive visits.

5. Camps
Prisoners confined to camps normally serve a sentence of 18 months or less and have not been convicted of a violent crime or sex offense.

Initially, work camps were located in remote rural locations. Living facilities were very rustic and consisted of multiple-occupancy cabins and one or more multipurpose buildings for showers, latrines, laundry, food service, religious services, indoor recreation, and visits. Inmates engaged in public works projects such as clearing brush, picking up trash along roadsides, constructing picnic grounds, and reforestation projects.

In the 1980s, a new form of camp styled after military basic-training boot camps emerged. The operational philosophy of a boot camp emphasizes strict discipline, regimentation, strenuous physical conditioning, hard physical labor, and military-style drills. Some boot camps provide educational and counseling programs at night.

Prisoners in boot camps dress in military-type fatigues, march in formation to and from activities, and are prohibited from speaking unless spoken to by camp personnel. The typical offender assigned to a boot camp is 17 to 25 years old and a first-time property offender.

6. Halfway Houses aka Transitional Living Centers
    As the name implies, a halfway house (transitional living center) houses prisoners who are nearing completion of a prison term and are moving from a higher-level security prison to the community.

    A halfway house is typically a single building similar in design and construction to a college dormitory or military barracks, and it is often located in or near a metropolitan area. The exterior doors are locked only at night to provide perimeter security. Unarmed personnel conduct random inspections inside the building and may conduct spot checks outside the building to ensure that all prisoners are accounted for.

Prisoners in a halfway house are allowed to leave the facility at any time during the day or night to go to an approved job, to attend school, or to participate in other authorized community-based programs intended to help the prisoner successfully transition from prison to the community.

Capital Punishment

While most of Europe, Canada, and dozens of other Western nations have abolished or stringently restricted the use of capital punishment during the last quarter of the 20th century, the US Congress and the legislative bodies of 38 states have enacted laws that authorize the use of capital punishment.

According to the Death Penalty Information Center, 1,463 criminals have been executed in the United States since 1976. The majority of the executions occurred in five states: Texas (544), Virginia (113), Oklahoma (112), Florida (94) and Missouri (88). Oregon has executed two criminals since 1976.

There is little debate about whether capital punishment is the ultimate form of punishment, although some argue that a life sentence without the possibility of parole is as punitive if not more punitive (Bedau 1997). There is seemingly no end to the arguments surrounding this practice. Chief among the topics debated, in addition to its effectiveness as a deterrent, are the legality of capital punishment, its morality, and its potential for discrimination.

Legality of Capital Punishment

Most challenges to the legality of capital punishment are based on the argument that it is a cruel and unusual form of punishment and therefore violates the Eighth Amendment to the Constitution: "Excessive bail shall not be required, nor excessive fines imposed, nor cruel and unusual punishment inflicted," says the Constitution.

Opponents argue the death penalty denies defendants equal protection under the law, which is guaranteed by the 14th Amendment.

Although the Supreme Court has never ruled that the death penalty violates the Eighth or 14th Amendment, the court did rule in 1972 that the death penalty is unconstitutional if the sentencing procedures do not make adequate provisions to prevent the arbitrary and capricious imposition of the penalty (Furman v. Georgia 408 U. S. 238).

The Supreme Court reaffirmed this decision in 1976 when it ruled the sentencing procedures used to impose the death penalty on Troy Gregg were sufficient to ensure the sentence was neither arbitrary nor capricious (Gregg v. Georgia 428 U. S. 153).

The Supreme Court upheld the use of hanging, firing squad, electric chair, and gas chamber. A decision regarding the use of lethal injection, currently the preferred method of execution, has not yet been ruled upon by the High Court. Until the Supreme Court rules otherwise or congressional action is taken declaring the death penalty illegal, it is legal.

Morality of Capital Punishment

Opponents of the death penalty argue that murder and execution are acts born out of hate, vengeance, anger, and resentment, and the government should not knowingly engage in such behavior. In effect, the government is symbolically condoning killing rather than conveying its rejection of the behavior (Bedau 1997). Those who support the morality of capital punishment justify it in the following ways.

1. Lawful Act

    According to those who support capital punishment, murder is statutorily defined as an "unlawful act" taken in malice by one human being against another. An execution is a "lawful action" taken without malice by the government, not by an individual, and therefore does not constitute murder.

2. Retribution

    Supporters also argue that an execution is retribution, not revenge and it differs from revenge in three critical ways.

    Retribution is taken in response to an established wrong. Actions taken in revenge or as retaliation are driven by a perceived wrong.

    Retribution is governed by strict limits, which have been established to ensure that the degree of punishment imposed is suitable to the crime. Actions taken in revenge have no boundaries to limit the extent or degree of punishment.

    Retribution is an impartial act taken to protect the interests of society as a whole, not for personal satisfaction, which is the motivation for actions taken in revenge (Cassell 2004; Judd 2003).

Some—such as theologian and philosopher Louis Pojman, coeditor of *Debating the Death Penalty: Should America Have Capital Punishment?*—support the use of the death penalty even though mistakes have and will continue to be made, mistakes that may have resulted, or may result, in the execution of an innocent person. Pojman argues the following:

> *Society has a right to protect itself from capital offenses even if this means taking a finite chance of executing an innocent person. Fire trucks occasionally kill innocent pedestrians while racing to fires, but we accept these losses as justified by the greater good of the activity of using fire trucks. We judge the use of automobiles to be acceptable even though such use causes an average 50,000 traffic fatalities each year. We accept the morality of a defensive war even though it will result in our troop's accidentally or mistakenly killing innocent people.*
>
> *That an occasional error may be made, regrettable though this is, is not a sufficient reason for us to refuse to use the death penalty, if on balance it serves a just and useful function. (Pojman 2004, p. 68)*

Although fire trucks may be involved in an accident while in route to a fire, the drivers do not knowingly drive with the understanding that an accident will occur while in route, and if the accident results in the death of an innocent bystander, the death is justified.

In all likelihood, an accident of this nature will be investigated, and the driver will be held accountable if found negligent in any way. Even if negligence is not found, the accident and the loss of an innocent life are not considered "justified" because some greater social good was being pursued. The same argument applies to auto accidents.

I am not certain what Pojman means by a "defensive war," but my understanding of the "rules of war" is that they require combat forces to make every effort to prevent casualties of innocent noncombatants. Combat forces at every level of the military hierarchy are held accountable when they fail to do so.

In the case of the death penalty, we purposely execute a human being while knowing innocent people have been convicted and executed for a crime they did not commit. The death of an innocent person by enacting the death penalty is not an accidental byproduct as it is in auto accidents or war—it is a tragedy. The purposeful death of an innocent human being is a criminal act.

Discrimination

Some opponents of the death penalty assert that racial minorities, particularly blacks and Hispanics, are more likely to be arrested, convicted, and executed for committing a capital crime than are whites (Bedau and Radelet 1987; Radelet et al. 1992; Huff et al. 1996; Westervelt and Humphrey 2001; Parker et al. 2003).

This assertion is based primarily on the analysis and interpretation of demographic data (gender, race, education level, and age) collected by the US Department of Justice in relation to persons sentenced to death or executed in the United States since 1977. It is also based on independent studies focused on specific factors such as the race of a person exonerated by new evidence after being convicted of a capital offense.

    THOMAS TOOMBS, PhD

Proponents of the death penalty dispute the assertion that capital punishment is discriminatory by challenging the validity and veracity of the opponents' data analysis, interpretation, and independent studies and by presenting their own (Cassell 2004; Wilbanks 1987; Langan 1976). The question of whether capital punishment is influenced by race remains subject to debate.

As unlikely as some want to believe, the results obtained by The Innocence Project indicate that the accidental execution of an innocent person is a real possibility. Established in 1992 by Barry Scheck (one of O. J. Simpson's defense attorneys) and Peter Neufeld, The Innocence Project is a national litigation and public policy organization dedicated to exonerating wrongfully convicted people through DNA testing. The project's website (innocenceproject.org) notes the following:

- There have been 297 post-conviction exonerations in the United States since the project was founded.

- Seventeen of the 297 people exonerated through DNA testing served time on death row, and another 15 exonerated people were charged with capital crimes but not sentenced to death.

- The average length of time served by those exonerated is 13 years. The total number of years served by the group of exonerated people is 3,944.

Positivist School Theories

Sociological Determinism
- Psychological Determinism
- Biological Determinism
- Sociobiology and Evolutionary Psychology
- Post-Traumatic Slavery Syndrome

Positivist school theorists believe criminal behavior is a product of factors over which the criminal has no control, not the product of free will, as classical school theorists proclaim. There is, however, no consensus within the positivist school about what the underlying factor(s) is that causes criminal behavior.

Some students of the school argue that criminal behavior is caused by biological factors—criminals are simply born with criminal tendencies. Others argue criminal behavior is the product of psychological trauma. Perhaps the most popular theory is that criminal behavior is the result of exposure to negative sociological factors in one's living environment over which the criminal has no control such as money, employment, education, health care, and housing.

Positivist school theorists—with the exception of theorists who attribute criminal behavior to brain structural abnormalities, sociobiology, and evolutionary psychology—believe criminals can be deterred from further criminal behavior through the process of rehabilitation.

The first step in the rehabilitation process is a comprehensive "needs assessment." After a criminal is convicted, he or she undergoes a medical/dental examination and a battery of psychological, academic, and vocational aptitude tests. In addition, a social history—which includes family history, work history, education history and prior criminal history—is collected and documented.

The needs assessment can be completed prior to sentencing, and the court can use it to decide whether to sentence the individual to a prison term or place the individual on probation. Alternatively, the needs assessment can be completed after the person is sentenced and incarcerated.

The results of the assessment are used to design a customized treatment plan. For example, an offender who is unable to read or write is enrolled in a remedial education program. One who does not have a high school diploma is enrolled in a GED program. One who has no employment skills is enrolled in a vocational training program. If the individual is a sex offender, or if testing and social history indicate that the person has a psychological problem or history of substance abuse, the person will be enrolled in an appropriate rehabilitation program.

Sociological Determinism

Classical school thinking went unchallenged until the essays of Auguste Comte, a French philosopher, were published in the mid-18th and early 19th centuries. Comte is considered by some to be the father of modern sociology.

Conte theorized that human intelligence passes through three stages: theological, metaphysical, and scientific. In the theological stage, human intelligence seeks to account for the world by seeing it as under the control of supernatural beings. In the metaphysical stage, human intelligence seeks an explanation for mysterious abstract forces (e.g., nature). In the scientific stage, the focus of human intelligence is discovering the empirical relationships between phenomena.

Comte's objective was to make sociology a science—like astronomy, physics, or chemistry—so that social problems could be solved objectively. According to Comte, examining social problems with a positivist philosophy showed that while certain wrongs were inevitable and others curable, it was foolish to try to cure the incurable in social as well as in biological and chemical matters. Comte's thinking led to the development of positivist school theories in the field of corrections (Thompson 1976; Harp 1995).

Although there is general agreement about what social factors promote criminal behavior (poverty, unemployment, substandard housing, hunger, poor health care, and illiteracy), there are a number of theories about how these factors interact to promote criminal behavior. The discussion that follows features seven of the more prominent sociological theories.

1. Cultural Deviance or Subculture Theory
    Among the early scholarly works to advance the culture deviance or subculture theory were those of Wolfgang and Ferracuti (1967), Cloward and Ohlin (1960), Cohen (1955), and Miller (1958). According to this theory, individuals who exhibit criminal behavior are typically reared in environments characterized by slum conditions: low income, racial and ethnic segregation, poor health care, high divorce rates, and elevated school drop-out rates. Such conditions breed a subculture with a deviant value system that is in conflict with the values of the law-abiding population.

2. Strain Theory
    The desire for money is the driving force behind strain theory. Proponents argue that when low-income

     THOMAS TOOMBS, PhD

individuals are unable to improve their economic status, they are forced to resort to criminal behavior (Agnew 2002).

3. Structural Theory

    Structural theory is a variation of strain theory. Its essence is that criminal behavior stems from the creation of false expectations. According to the theory, children in America are raised to believe that anyone can become president or a millionaire, but the reality is that the structure of society permits only a select few to achieve such goals. The frustration generated when confronted with the reality that equal opportunity is a myth results in criminal behavior (Merton 1996).

4. Social Control Theory

    Social control theory asserts that human beings are antisocial by nature. Noncriminals learn to control their antisocial instincts through association with and instruction from others in society who believe in and respect the law (parents, teachers, friends, clergy, coaches, and so on). Individuals who grow up without the benefit of these positive influences are more likely to engage in criminal activity regardless of their socioeconomic background, education, or family history (Hirschi 1969).

5. Social Disorganization Theory

    This theory was advanced by French sociologist Emile Durkheim in the late 1890s. Durkheim postulated that societies develop through a two-stage process. In the first phase (the mechanical phase), people are more homogenous. They perform basically the same work, live by a common set of rules, and think and behave alike. In the second phase (the organic phase), life is more complex, and people are more diverse. There is less of a sense of community, and people no longer share a cultural bond.

Deviant behavior, including criminal behavior, occurs when the norms and behavioral expectations by which people live are undefined, confused, or unclear. Social control, which is a byproduct of shared goals and norms, ceases to exist. Durkheim referred to this condition as anomie (Alexander and Smith 2005).

In the 1920s, George H. Mead, Ellsworth Faris, Herbert Blumer, and Robert Park, faculty members at the University of Chicago department of sociology, refined Durkheim's concept into what became known as the Chicago school of empirical sociology. The Chicago School's approach was to move the study of human beings from the classroom to where people lived and worked. The principal thesis of the Chicago school's philosophy is that human beings were innately social creatures, and as such, their behavior was the product of their social environment. Through direct observation, Chicago-school investigators concluded that as a result of urbanization, industrialization, and mass migration into inner cities, the basic institutions of society—family, friendships, and other social groups—fragmented, creating separate groups and communities with conflicting norms and value systems. Absent a common value system, multiple, diverse groups with conflicting values formed, fostering an array of social problems including criminal activity.

6. Labeling Theory

   According to this theory, criminal behavior is neither right nor wrong. "Criminal behavior" is a label attached to any behavior that deviates from the norm as defined by people with power—parents, teachers, judges, and lawmakers—in an attempt to shame the individual into conformity.

   Two things happen when behavior is labeled: the individual is stigmatized and shunned by nondeviant members of society, and the individual adopts the labeled behavior as a lifestyle.

   All human beings need to feel accepted. Unable to find acceptance in mainstream society, the "criminal" finds it through association with others similarly labeled. The individual takes on the role and lifestyle he or she has been assigned and abandons any attempt to conform to social norms.

   Frank Tannenbaum (*Crime and the Community*, 1938), Edwin Lemert (*Social Pathology: A Systematic Approach to the Theory of Sociopathic Behavior*, 1951), and Howard Becker (*Outsiders: Studies in the Sociology of Deviance*, 1963) were among the notable early proponents of labeling theory. Referring to labeling as the "dramatization of evil," Tannenbaum said that labeling evokes the very behavior it finds offensive. In the end, the individuals become what they have previously been accused of being.

   Lemert characterized the process of labeling as the "societal reaction approach," which manifested in two different forms of deviance: primary and secondary.

Primary deviance occurs when an individual behaves—for sociological, psychological, or biological reasons that are beyond his or her control—in a way that is considered deviant. Secondary deviance forms as a defensive reaction in response to society's reaction to primary deviance.

Becker believed that most people harbor deviant thoughts. Most control their thoughts and do not act out their deviance, while others were unable or unwilling to control their thoughts and act them out.

According to Becker, labeling is a three-step process. The initial and most crucial step occurs the moment an individual is first caught and assigned the label of criminal by a higher authority. The second step occurs when the individual surrenders to the consensus, accepts the assigned label, and begins to view himself or herself as a criminal. The third step occurs when the individual fully adopts the role of a criminal and makes it a lifestyle.

7. Reintegrative Shaming aka Restorative Justice Theory

The concept of reintegrative shaming was proposed in the late 1980s by John Braithwaite, a professor in the law program at the Research School of Social Sciences at Australian National University and author of *Crime, Shame, and Reintegration*. A form of labeling theory, reintegrative shame theory argues that labeling can serve as a catalyst for positive change if the focus is placed on condemning the offensive behavior rather than on condemning the offender.

 THOMAS TOOMBS, PhD

The objectives of the traditional criminal justice system, according to reintegrative shame theorists, are to determine what law was broken, identify who broke it, and punish violators. The process is built on the premise that if the focus is restoration as opposed to retribution, shame can invoke remorse. This can allow a person to accept responsibility for bad behavior and lead him or her to refrain from blaming others. Theoretically, restorative shame will give satisfaction to the victims of the crime, because the objective is to reintegrate the criminal into mainstream society, not to ostracize the person (Braithwaite 1989).

Psychological Determinism

The concept of psychological determinism was introduced in 1863 by Cesare Lombroso in *Criminal Man*. The essence of this theory is that human behavior is determined by the interaction of biological and psychological factors specific to an individual's living situation.

1. Psychotic Disorders

    In the simplest terms, psychotic disorders are characterized by one's inability to distinguish right from wrong or to differentiate fantasy from reality. Hallucinations— auditory, visual, or both—are common indicators of psychotic behavior. If an individual commits a crime and is found to have been psychotic at the time, he or she will likely be found not responsible due to a mental disease or defect or not guilty by reason of insanity.

    In lieu of being punished, offenders diagnosed as psychotic are normally placed in a hospital for the mentally ill. They remain hospitalized until a court examines reports from the attending psychiatrist and determines that the mental illness is in remission and the person no longer constitutes a threat to others if released. Some states, such as Oregon, have established an independent board to review psychiatrists' recommendations and make the decision to release the individual or order him or her to continue inpatient treatment (MacKay 1995).

2. Neurotic Disorders
    Neurotic disorders characteristically involve extreme anxiety triggered by an unfounded fear or threat, physical complaints for which there is no known cause, or obsessive thoughts and compulsive acts that drastically interfere with normal life. People with compulsive disorders, for example, may spend hours washing their hands after going to the bathroom in response to obsessive and irrational thoughts about bacterial disease (Martin 1971).

3. Personality Disorders
    The American Psychiatric Association (APA) generic definition of a personality disorder is "an enduring pattern of inner experience and behavior that deviates markedly from the expectation of the individual's culture, is pervasive and inflexible, has an onset in adolescence or early adulthood, is stable over time and leads to distress or impairment." There are ten distinct disorders: Antisocial Personality Disorder, Avoidant Personality Disorder, Borderline Personality Disorder, Dependent Personality Disorder, Histrionic Personality Disorder, Narcissistic Personality Disorder, Obsessive-Compulsive Personality

Disorder, Paranoid Personality Disorder, Schizoid Personality Disorder, and Schizotype Personality Disorder (American Psychiatric Association 2010).

Most criminals are classified as having an antisocial personality disorder and display traits that are sometimes called psychopathic or sociopathic. A person with an antisocial personality disorder is often manipulative, impulsive, deceitful and possesses no sense of remorse. He or she shows little or no regard for laws, rules, or the rights of others and is unable or unwilling to sustain personal relationships with friends, family, employers, or coworkers unless it is profitable to do so (Meloy 1988).

The general public and the media often mistakenly use the terms *psychotic* and *psychopathic* interchangeably because it is hard for a rational person to understand how a human being could knowingly commit a criminal act, particularly a brutal act of violence, unless the offender is psychotic and does not understand what he or she is doing. Psychopaths are not psychotic. Psychopaths know what they are doing and whether what they are doing is right or wrong. They simply don't care.

Those who believe that criminal behavior is psychologically determined usually advocate some form of psychotherapy. There are multiple types, but the approaches most commonly used are psychoanalysis-psychodynamic therapy, interpersonal therapy, and cognitive behavioral therapy (George 1990).

1. Psychoanalysis-Psychodynamic Therapy
    The premise of this therapy is that abnormal behavior is
    the product of conflict between an individual's defense
    mechanisms and unwanted memories of bad childhood
    experiences hidden in an individual's subconscious mind.

    Based on theories Sigmund Freud proposed in the late
    19th century, the remedy or treatment for abnormal
    behavior is to release these hidden feelings from
    the subconscious through conversation, a process
    sometimes called "talk therapy."

    Through dialogue, a psychotherapist attempts to help
    patients understand the origin of their inner conflict
    and the feelings generated by it. The theory is that once
    the individual understands these feelings, the conflict
    will subside, and the abnormal behavior it is causing
    becomes more susceptible to change (Corey 1991).

2. Interpersonal Therapy
    Interpersonal therapy is similar to psychoanalytic-
    psychodynamic therapy in that it also involves an
    ongoing conversation between a therapist and a patient.
    Interpersonal therapy focuses the conversation on current
    events that may be the underlying causes of the person's
    behavioral problems such as the death of a loved one,
    unwanted or unexpected employment status changes,
    geographical relocation, or marital or family conflict (Ivey
    et al. 2002).

3. Cognitive Behavioral Therapy
    Cognitive behavioral therapy is based on the idea that
    behavior is the product of conscious beliefs and perceptions,

                    THOMAS TOOMBS, PhD

not unconscious conflicts caused by traumatic early life experiences. How a person feels and behaves is the result of how the person thinks, not external events or the actions of other people.

Criminal behavior occurs as a result of "thinking errors" that originate in false perceptions and irrational beliefs. The individual's mistaken perception of life's events, as opposed to the events themselves, generate erroneous thinking, which results in behavior that is unacceptable, destructive, and harmful to the person, others, or both (Anderson 1995).

Unlike psychodynamic and interpersonal therapies, which are fluid, flexible, and open-ended, cognitive behavioral therapy, although collaborative, is highly structured and more goal-directed, with the patient and therapist performing interdependent but different roles.

The goal is to identify and eliminate the errors in a person's thought processes and replace them with those that produce more desirable feelings and behavior. The therapist's role is to listen, teach, and encourage. The patient's role is to speak, learn, and implement what is learned.

Cognitive behavioral therapy is typically much shorter than psychoanalytical therapy. It lasts weeks, or perhaps months in more complex cases, as opposed to the many years a course of psychoanalytical therapy might last.

In the mid-1990s, Samuel Yochelson and Stanton Samenow coauthored *The Criminal Personality, Volume I: A Profile for Change* (1994) and *Criminal*

Personality, Volume II: The Change Process (1995). These publications are the culmination of a 14-year study conducted by the authors as part of the Program for the Investigation of Criminal Behavior at St. Elizabeth's Hospital, a division of the National Institute of Mental Health in Washington, DC.

Yochelson, who started the study, was seeking to discover what causes criminal behavior and to determine how the behavior could be changed using traditional psychotherapeutic techniques. After four years, Yochelson concluded that he had made no progress toward finding a cause. He also concluded that traditional psychotherapeutic methods were not only ineffective for dealing with criminal behavior but were also based on an incorrect premise that criminal behavior, like all behavior, is learned through life experiences.

After reviewing the results from the first four years of the study, Yochelson and Samenow came to the conclusion that criminal behavior is a rational choice made on the basis of irrational thinking ("thinking errors") and that attributing the origins of criminal behavior to unfortunate life experiences—whether psychological or social—allows criminals to justify their behavior and blame others for who they are and what they do (Yochelson and Samenow 1994).

Abandoning the goal of finding a cause for criminal behavior, Yochelson and Samenow started a new study based on the premise that criminal behavior is the combined result of specific personality traits and a particular thinking process.

According to the researchers, criminals are manipulative, restless, dissatisfied, irritable, selfish, demanding, coercive, scheming, and driven by an insatiable need for excitement and self-satisfaction, no matter what the cost. Criminals believe that rules and laws are for others. Criminals view people (family and friends included) as objects whose needs, wants, and expectations are impositions to be ignored unless they serve the criminal's interest.

Yochelson and Samenow concluded that for criminals to change, they must be shown the errors in their thinking and taught new ways of thinking. However, before criminals can be taught how to change, they must reach the conclusion that change will be beneficial, which will most likely not happen until they hit rock bottom.

Out of the 255 participants that started the program, only 30 followed it to completion, and only nine demonstrated signs of genuine change as Yochelson and Samenow chose to measure it. Their best estimate was that the cognitive behavioral approach would benefit no more than 20 percent of the criminal population, which was no better than the recidivism rate for criminals who spend an unspecified term in prison, unexposed to any form of treatment (Samenow 2002; Yochelson and Samenow 1995).

Biological Determinism

"Criminals are born, not made" claim those who believe that biological factors produce criminal behavior. Exactly how criminals differ biologically from noncriminals—and whether the biological anomalies are random mutations, genetic flaws that are passed along from one generation to another, or selected genes that are acquired and passed along—is a matter of debate within this group.

1. Bodily Fluids

    The origin of the idea that behavioral differences between people are attributable to inherent differences in physiological makeup can be traced back to the theories of Hippocrates, a Greek physician born in 460 BC. Hippocrates is known as the "Father of Medicine" and the author of the Hippocratic Oath to which all physicians swear allegiance.

    Hippocrates postulated that humans possess four bodily fluids called humors—yellow bile, black bile, blood, and phlegm—in varying amounts. The relative concentrations the humors in the body results, according to the theory, in different pairs of body qualities: warm versus cool and dry versus moist. The relative balance among these qualities, said Hippocrates, is what produces variations in behavior between people (Jones 1931).

    Hippocrates' explanation for individual differences in behavior remained the standard until the second century AD, when Claudius Galen, another Greek physician and considered by many to be the next most important contributor to classical medicine after Hippocrates, expanded on his predecessor's thinking. According to Galen, a person's temperament fits into one of four categories:

The melancholic temperament, which characteristically involves sadness or depression, is caused by excess black bile.

The sanguine temperament, which describes one who is warm and pleasant, is caused by excess blood.

The choleric temperament, which is fiery and hot-tempered, is caused by excess yellow bile.

The phlegmatic temperament, categorizing one who is apathetic and slovenly, is caused by excess phlegm (Kagen 1994).

2. Physiognomy and Phrenology

    Giambattista della Porta, a 14th-century Italian physician, proposed the concept of physiognomy. According to Giambattista, a person's character could be discovered by interpreting his or her outward appearance—especially the features of the face—rather than by measuring the relative balance of the four humors. For example, large, protruding facial features—particularly the nose, lips, and jaw—were suggested to be indicators of a criminal character (Jenkins 1997).

In the early 19th century, Franz Gall, a Viennese physician, proposed the concept of phrenology. The premise of phrenology is that the brain is comprised of multiple distinct areas that determine an individual's personality, intellect, disposition, and aptitudes, among other things.

Gall claimed that as the skull forms, the shape and size of each area in the brain creates indentations and bumps on the outer surface of the skull. By running one's fingers and palms over the skull, one could supposedly interpret the bumps and the indentations, thus revealing an individual's personality, disposition, character, psychological traits, and intellectual aptitudes (Van Wyne 2003; Sabbatini 1997).

3. Atavism

In the late 19th century, Cesare Lombroso, an Italian psychiatrist who had been strongly influenced by Darwin's theory of evolution, proposed that criminals were an atavism in the evolutionary chain, a throwback to a lower form of life with physical features and social traits similar to those of apes.

Lombroso observed that criminals typically have long arms, large ears, flat noses, fat lips, high cheekbones, strongly defined canine teeth, protruding jaws, extraordinary strength, and better-than-average agility. According to Lombroso, criminals manifest the behavior of a savage animal and lack the ability to restrain or control their behavior (Gibson 2002).

Although Lombroso acknowledged that some crimes were committed out of rage, passion, or desperation, he argued that "to understand crime one must study the criminal, not his rearing, not his education, not the current predicament that might have inspired his theft and pillage" (Gould's *The Mismeasure of Man*, p. 126).

In an attempt to legitimize his theory, Lombroso documented massive amounts of statistical data, which he used to manufacture mathematical formulas designed to justify his positions. After undergoing intense scrutiny by the likes of Paul Broca and Paul

Topinard—physicians and pioneers in the fields of anthropology and neurology—Lombroso and his discoveries eventually lost all credibility.

4. Somatotyping or Body Typing

In the early 20th century, German psychiatrist Ernst Kretschmer offered another biological theory that he called somatotyping or body typing. Later expanded upon by American psychologist William Sheldon, and Eleanor and Sheldon Glueck of the Harvard Law faculty, somatotyping is similar to physiognomy and phrenology in that it is more a method of identifying criminals than a means of explaining the etiology of criminal behavior or of preventing criminal behavior.

According to Kretschmer, Sheldon, and the Gluecks, all humans have one of three body types. Kretschmer labeled them asthenic, athletic, and pyknic. The Gluecks used the terms endomorph, mesomorph, and ectomorph. Each body type was associated with a different mental disorder or behavioral pattern. It was the view of Kretschmer, Sheldon, and the Gluecks that criminals have an athletic or mesomorphic body type (Arrai 1994; Glueck 1956; Kretschmer 1949).

- The asthenic or endomorphic type is characterized by wide hips, narrow shoulders, large wrists and ankles, and excessive fat on the body, upper arms, and thighs.

- The athletic or mesomorphic type is characterized by broad shoulders and narrow hips, a muscular body, very little fat, and strong forearms, calves, and thighs.

- The pyknic or ectomorphic type is characterized by narrow shoulders, hips, and chest, a thin face, a high forehead, very little muscle or fat, and thin legs and arms.

5. Diet

Improper diet or vitamin deficiency is also theorized to link criminal behavior to biological/physiological factors. Those who promote this idea have identified foods they claim are directly linked to criminal behavior. Others argue evidence suggests there is a strong link between deficiencies in vitamins and minerals and criminal behavior.

In addition to the elimination of certain foods from the diet—specifically, foods containing refined sugar or white flour, foods with a high caloric content, dairy products, and citrus fruits—other suggested nutritional remedies include measured doses of vitamins, minerals, and special health foods. Most common among the recommended vitamins and minerals are niacin, pantothenic acid, thiamine, vitamin B6 and C, folate, iron, magnesium, and amino acids.

In 1988, the National Institute of Corrections commissioned the RAND Corporation to survey the literature on the most prominent behavioral science and nutrition studies that had been designed to explore the relationship between diet and criminal behavior. The studies reviewed included those that had concluded that diet significantly influences behavior and those that concluded that diet does not have a significant effect on behavior.

Diana Fishbein and Susan Pease authored a report titled "The Effects of Diet on Behavior: Implications for Criminology and Corrections." Fishbein and Pease concluded that because the studies they reviewed had not been conducted in accordance with the fundamental principles of scientific investigation, none of the studies had produced sufficient empirical evidence to either support or refute the argument that diet has a significant impact on behavior.

In 2002, the *British Journal of Psychiatry* published the results of an 18-month study designed and conducted by Oxford University scientist C. Bernard Gesch. It assessed the influence of supplementary vitamins, minerals, and essential fatty acids on the antisocial behavior of young adult prisoners.

The experiment was a double-blind, placebo-controlled trial involving 231 randomly selected prisoners in a maximum security prison in England. The aim was to test the effects of supplements containing vitamins, minerals, and essential fatty acids on prisoner behavior by comparing the disciplinary records of the participating prisoners before, during, and after the test. Half of the study group was randomly selected to unknowingly receive the diet supplement, and the other half unknowingly received the placebo.

When the results for each group were compared, the group taking the dietary supplements received an average of 26.3 percent fewer misconduct reports than the group taking the placebo. When compared to their baseline data, the results showed that the group taking the supplements committed 35.1 percent fewer conduct violations, while the rate of misconduct for the placebo group remained virtually unchanged. Gesch and his colleagues readily admitted that the results of their research were correlative only and advised others not to make generalized conclusions about criminal behavior on the basis of their findings.

6. Brain Disorders

The development of electromagnetic and digital imaging devices and techniques has created more reliable and graphic methods for exploring the structure of the brain and determining with more certainty how it works. Recent studies have led investigators to conclude that there may be a relationship between criminal behavior—particularly violent behavior—and structural abnormalities in the prefrontal cortex and the medial temporal lobes, which are the areas of the brain thought to be responsible for impulse control, judgment, planning, remorse, concern for others, and concern for the consequences of one's actions (Bufkin and Luttrell 2005; Raine et al. 2000).

Structural Abnormality

Scientists have determined that the brain is comprised of four distinct sections—the brain stem, the midbrain or cerebellum, the limbic system, and the cerebral cortex—and that each section controls different bodily functions and physical and mental abilities.

The brain stem controls essential functions such as heart rate, blood pressure, and temperature. The midbrain or cerebellum is responsible for controlling appetite and sleep. The limbic system controls emotions such as pleasure, joy, anger, sadness, and remorse. The cerebral cortex is subdivided into four lobes: the occipital, which controls vision; the parietal, which controls the sense of touch and spatial understanding; the temporal, which controls hearing and language; and the frontal, which regulates movement, planning, reasoning, memory, self-control, attention, and judgment (DSQUIC 2000). As scientists learned more about how the brain works, they gained insight into how a bodily function or behavior is affected when the area in the brain that is responsible for controlling a particular function or behavior is rendered dysfunctional through injury, illness, or incomplete or incorrect development at birth.

A coalition of medical researchers in Los Angeles and San Francisco observed and compared the behavior of Alzheimer patients with that of patients known to have prefrontal cortex damage. They found that both groups manifested unacceptable behavior that is characteristic of sociopaths such as unsolicited sexual acts, physical assaults, and lack of remorse (Mendez et al. 2005).

Chemical Imbalance

The theory that criminal behavior can be caused by an imbalance of chemicals within the brain could be characterized as a modern-day version of Hippocrates' and Galen's theories. The difference is that Hippocrates and Galen attributed behavioral differences to the relative balance of blood, bile, and phlegm rather than to the balance of brain chemicals, which were unknown at the time.

Proponents of this theory claim to have identified more than 50 chemical substances in the brain, which they call neurotransmitters. The function of a neurotransmitter is to transmit messages between components of the brain as well as messages from the brain to other parts of the body. The type and level of neurotransmitters in any given brain ostensibly determine the message that is communicated and the message's intensity. In theory, maintaining a proper balance of chemicals in the brain can prevent problematic behavior just as regulating other chemicals and substances in the body can prevent or control high blood pressure, high cholesterol, or diabetes.

Medical research into the human genome may offer the greatest promise for discovering what causes human beings to commit crime. The identification of a genetic link to criminal behavior would explain what no other theories offered to date can: why one of two individuals reared in the same environment, exposed to the same psycho-socio-economic trauma, and eating the same food becomes a criminal while the other does not?

Sociobiology and Evolutionary Psychology

Two of the more recent biologically based theories advanced by the positivist school are sociobiology and evolutionary psychology. The premise of both theories is the same; they differ only in their focus.

According to sociobiologists and evolutionary psychologists, the primary behavioral features of every human being, like the primary physical traits of every living organism, evolved by adapting to the environment and are stored in the genes.

The major difference between the two theories is that the former is focused exclusively on understanding the behavior of humans, whereas the latter explores the behavior of all living organisms.

Adaptation in the evolutionary process is based on the biological principle that the physical characteristics of contemporary animals—wings on birds, hands on humans, hoofs on horses, and gills on fish—are a direct result of their ancestors having adapted to a problem that threatened their survival.

Applied to human behavior, adaptation is the belief that phenol typical behavior (behavior that is readily observable in humans from the earliest stages of life) can also be traced to the ancestral need for behavioral change that would have enhanced the evolutionary prospects of the species.

In 1975, Edward O. Wilson—a zoologist at Harvard University, winner of two Pulitzer prizes, and world-renowned for his study of animal behavior, particularly that of ants—postulated that all animal behavior, including human behavior, is physiologically based in a genetic structure that evolved through the same natural selection process as that through which physical characteristics are acquired, as described by Charles Darwin.

Wilson borrowed the term "sociobiology" from John P. Scott, a pioneer researcher in behavioral genetics, and called it "a new discipline." Wilson says sociobiology is

> *a more explicitly hybrid discipline that incorporates knowledge from ethnology (the naturalistic study of whole patterns of behavior), ecology (the study of the relationships of organisms to their environment), and genetics in to order to derive general principles concerning the biological properties of entire societies. (Wilson, Sociobiology and Human Nature, 1978)*

Wilson acknowledged that some behavior is learned, to a degree, through environmental influences, but he believed that the basic features of human behavior—a tendency toward hierarchy, a deep personal concern about status and recognition, a tendency to place great value on self-esteem and individual integrity, a desire for personal privacy, a desire for deep sexual bonding and deep parental bonding, an aversion to incestuous behavior, and a tendency toward tribalism—is "hardwired" into the genes, just like the basic physical traits that have helped humans to survive. Wilson believes that behaviors such as altruism, sexism, racism, selfishness, crime, aggression, and violence developed through the process of natural selection over millions of years.

As might be expected, the idea that human behavior is a product of evolution has not been met without controversy. It has prompted a storm of fiery written exchanges, in the form of books and journal articles, between supporters and critics of evolutionary psychology and sociobiology. In addition to criticism from creationists who oppose any idea about the origin of life that conflicts with the Bible, the underlying principles of sociobiology and evolutionary psychology are also criticized on political and scientific grounds.

Political objections to sociobiology and evolutionary psychology form around the concern that those who promote these concepts are motivated by a hidden agenda: to maintain the status quo and perpetuate a belief system that fosters and sustains racism, sexism, classism, and similar discriminatory ideologies and types of behavior.

Critics of evolution-based theory point out that a similar attraction to genetics during the Nazi era in Germany led to the formulation and implementation of eugenic policies and practices that resulted in the annihilation of six million Jews. Others fear that wholesale adoption of the belief that behavior is genetically based may be used to reinforce the view that blacks are more predisposed to commit crime than whites.

Post-Traumatic Slavery Syndrome

One positivist school theory that does not to fit under any of the previously cited categories is post-traumatic slavery syndrome.

Black scholars such as Alvin Poussaint, Joy DeGruy-Leary, Amy Alexander, Omar G. Reid, Sekou Mims, and Larry Higginbottom assert that higher rates of crime, unemployment, suicide, and drug-use among blacks are attributable to what they called "post-traumatic slavery syndrome."

DeGruy-Leary, an assistant professor in the School of Social Work at Portland State University (and self-proclaimed originator of the post-traumatic slavery syndrome theory) attributes the syndrome to traumas such as experiencing or observing serious physical harm or the threat of serious physical harm, experiencing or observing torture or a kidnapping, or witnessing a person being killed, experienced during slavery that were not properly addressed through therapy (DeGruy-Leary 2005).

Others such as Alvin Poussaint, coauthor with Amy Alexander of *Lay My Burden Down: Unraveling Suicide and the Mental Health Crisis among African-Americans* (2000), assert that post-traumatic slavery syndrome is caused by the accumulating effects of being the victim of persistent racism, poverty, discrimination, and lack of quality health care.

Although Poussaint fails to adequately explain exactly how the effects of trauma experienced by slaves is transmitted to subsequent generations, DeGruy-Leary says that it is adaptive behavior (learned) passed from one generation to another. Slave parents passed along to their children behaviors they used to adapt to the slave world in which they lived. Even though slavery no longer exists, members of the current generation still employ the adapted behavior.

LESSON 2:
Corrections Research Is Pseudoscientific

Corrections Research Is Pseudoscientific

Many academicians assert that the policies and practices of the criminal justice system are based on theories derived from scientific research (Giordano 2014.) The reality is criminal justice policies and practices are based on hunches, conjecture, guesswork and speculation derived from intuition, imagination and pseudo-scientific research.

The literature is replete with results of research and evaluation studies completed on an array of different crime prevention programs, but most of the research and evaluation was unsystematic and lacked rigor. The results of the majority of these studies are invalid and unreliable, because the methods used to conduct them failed to comply with the standards required in scientific inquiry. Research practices can and must be elevated beyond this level. The achievement of a higher level of research practice in corrections will require much greater diligence and discipline on the part of researchers.

Researchers must ensure compliance with the protocols governing research on human beings, and they must meet the requirements of the scientific method. Failure to do so will perpetuate pseudoscientific research, which will continue to produce results that contribute little or nothing toward discovering what causes criminal behavior and how to prevent it. Without better research, corrections policy and practice will continue to be based on myths, intuition, and the prerogatives of power.

In fairness, it should be noted that research involving human subjects is highly scrutinized and tightly controlled by government regulations and ethical standards self-imposed by researchers—significantly more so than research not involving human subjects.

In the United States, the federal government and most state governments have codified laws and promulgated regulations to govern human subject research. Similar regulations have been adopted in many foreign countries. In addition to government regulation, every reputable public and private university and research institution, and every professional discipline engaged in human subject research, has voluntarily adopted ethical standards of practice to govern the conduct of all persons involved.

The intent of these regulations and standards is to protect the rights of participants and to ensure that they have not been coerced into participating. These regulations are even more stringent if the subjects of the research are prisoners.

Prisoners are considered a vulnerable category, along with children, pregnant women, and people with mental or physical disabilities. They are vulnerable because the constraints of incarceration could affect their ability to make a truly voluntary decision regarding participation in the research.

Conducting scientific experiments on primates for the benefit of the humans is legal and socially acceptable within limits, although it does encounter protest. Conducting scientific research on human beings is theoretically legal but extremely difficult—and justifiably so—because of the safeguards built into the protocols governing the practice. These safeguards are necessary to prevent abuse and to guarantee the rigors of the scientific method, which are essential if researchers are to ensure that their results are objective and valid.

If the community of scholars engaged in criminal justice research want the public and governing bodies to listen to what they have to say about criminal behavior, if they want policies and practices adopted based on their findings, and if they want the media to be more objective and less sensational in reporting about crime, they must fully comply with the protocols governing acceptable research. They have to offer more than just correlative evidence to support their findings.

Inferring that a high correlation (either negative or positive) between two factors establishes a causal relationship is erroneous. Unfortunately, all research conducted to date into what causes criminal behavior has revealed nothing more than correlative evidence. Few researchers—particularly social-science researchers—acknowledge this fact.

The use of correlative evidence, in part, helps sustain the argument between classical and positivist schools over what causes criminal behavior and how to prevent it; and helps perpetuate myths, intuitive beliefs, and mistaken ideas.

If the field of criminology hopes to mature to the level of a true discipline or science, it must reconcile its diversity of thought. There must be what Edward O. Wilson refers to as "consilience" or unity of knowledge.

Most of the issues that vex humanity daily (ethnic conflict, arms escalation, overpopulation, abortion, environment, endemic poverty, [and crime])...cannot be solved without integrating knowledge from the natural sciences with that of the social sciences and humanities.

The crucial difference between [medical science and social science] is consilience. The medical sciences have it and the social sciences do not.

Medical scientists build upon a coherent foundation of molecular and cell biology. They pursue elements of health and illness all the way down to the level of biophysical chemistry. The success of their individual projects depends on the fidelity of their experimental design to fundamental principles, which the researchers endeavor to make consistent across all levels of biological organization from the whole organism down, step by step, to the molecule.

In contrast, "...the efforts of social scientists are snarled by disunity and a failure of vision. The reason for the confusion is...because "social scientists spurn the idea of the hierarchical ordering of knowledge that unites and drives the natural sciences. Split into independent cadres [social scientists]...seldom speak the same technical language from one specialty to the next. (Wilson 1999, pp. 13 and 198)

Some—perhaps many—social scientists might take issue with Wilson over whether medical science is as pure and harmonious as Wilson depicts it. The ongoing dispute between medical scientists over whether chemical imbalance in the brain is a valid concept, for example, is

 THOMAS TOOMBS, PhD

an indication that not all is well among the descendants of Hippocrates and Galen.

There should be no disagreement, however, over whether there is a need to unify the knowledge developed by the various schools of thought about what causes criminal behavior and how it can be prevented. Until then, no meaningful progress will be made toward isolating the cause and identifying solutions.

LESSON 3:
Neither Punishment nor Rehabilitation Effectively Deter Criminal Behavior

Neither Punishment nor Rehabilitation Effectively Deter Criminal Behavior

The effectiveness of corrections programs have been measured using a variety of methods including recidivism analysis, program specific analysis, meta analysis, and logic analysis. No matter what the method, the results do not suggest correctional programs, past or present, effectively deter criminal behavior.

Methods of Measuring Effectiveness in Corrections

1. Recidivism Analysis

Recidivism rates are the most common method used to measure the effectiveness of corrections programs. They are calculated by measuring the amount of time that elapses until a convicted criminal resumes criminal activity after a definitive point in time (such as being placed on probation, released from incarceration, or completing a self-improvement program).

The parameters used to measure the length of time, as well as the event used to demark failure, vary from state to state and the federal government.

The time frame for the calculation of some recidivism rates in some jurisdictions is three years; for others, five years. Still others use 90 or 180 days. An offender is considered a recidivist only if he or she fails within the time frame established to monitor their behavior. If the offender reoffends after this period has elapsed, he or she is not counted as a recidivist.

In some jurisdictions, the event used to signify failure is arrest. In other jurisdictions, reconviction is used. Still others use a return to prison as the triggering event. No jurisdiction follows an offender or group of offenders for the duration of their lives after release from prison, parole, or probation.

Recidivism Rates for Probation

In 2016, the U. S. Bureau of Justice Statistics released the results of a study in which it evaluated the success of 43,000 criminals placed on probation from 2005 to 2010. The results indicated 18 percent of the population was rearrested at least once in one year; 35 percent was rearrested at least once in three years, and 43 percent was rearrested at least once in five years.

The State of Oregon measures recidivism for probationers in three ways: those who are reincarcerated for committing a new felony within three years after being placed on probation, those who are convicted of a new misdemeanor or felony crime within three years after being placed on probation, and those arrested for a new crime within three years.

According to statistics provided by the Oregon State Criminal Justice Commission, the success rate or recidivism rate for criminals sentenced to probation in Oregon during the first six months of 2012 was as follows:

- 12 percent were incarcerated for a new felony crime within three years.

- 39 percent were convicted of a new misdemeanor or felony crime within three years.

- 46 percent were arrested for a new crime within three years.

Recidivism Rates for Prisons

Every prison, no matter what type, has basically one function: to maintain custody and control of the inmates and to prevent the inmates from committing criminal acts harmful to law-abiding citizens in the community. Some prisons attempt to fulfill a second function: offer inmates the opportunity through self-help programs to develop new behavior patterns that will help them avoid committing criminal acts when released. This second function is commonly known as the process of rehabilitation.

There can be no doubt prisons perform the first function very well. In spite of the publicity surrounding some escapes, the rate of escape from a confinement facility, nationally, was 10.5 per 10,000 inmates in 2013. The majority of these escapes are more appropriately called "walk-aways" because they occurred at a non-enclosed facility with minimal supervision. The data for Oregon suggest even better performance. According to Oregon's Department of Corrections, since 2001, there has been an average of 5 walk-aways per month from working outside a facility, nine escapes per year from facilities without a secure perimeter, and eight escapes per year from facilities with a secure perimeter.

Like it does with probation, the State of Oregon uses recidivism rates to measure the effectiveness of incarceration. As explained earlier, recidivism rates are calculated by measuring the amount of time that elapses until a person resumes criminal activity after a definitive point in time such as being placed on probation, released from incarceration, or completing a self-improvement program. The amount of time used to earmark success varies from state to state as well as the federal government.

Recidivism for a confinement facility in Oregon is measured in three ways: those reincarcerated for a new felony within three years of release on parole, those convicted of a new misdemeanor or felony within three years of release on parole, and those arrested for a new crime within three years of release on parole.

According to Oregon's Criminal Justice Commission, the success rate or recidivism rate for those released from prison or from a felony jail sentence in the first six months of 2012 was as follows:

- 17 percent were reincarcerated for a new felony within three years of release.

- 40 percent were convicted of a new misdemeanor or felony within three years of release.

- 53 percent were arrested for a new crime within three years of release.

According to Federal Bureau of Justice Statistics studies, researchers found the following:

- Within three years of release, about two-thirds (67.8 percent) of released prisoners were rearrested.

- Within five years of release, about three-quarters (76.6 percent) of released prisoners were rearrested.

- Of those prisoners who were rearrested, more than half (56.7 percent) were arrested by the end of the first year.

- Property offenders were the most likely to be rearrested, with 82.1 percent of released property offenders arrested for a new crime compared with 76.9 percent of drug offenders, 73.6 percent of public order offenders, and 71.3 percent of violent offenders.

Recidivism Rates for Capital Punishment

There is no question that the criminal who is executed will never commit another crime, but whether others are dissuaded from committing murder out of fear that they too will be executed is highly questionable.

The debate about whether the death penalty is an effective deterrent centers on whether executing one criminal for murder deters others from committing murder.

Isaac Ehrlich, distinguished professor of economics department at the University of Buffalo in New York State, was one of the first scholars to use statistical methods to calculate the effect of capital punishment on murder rates. Using the techniques of cost-benefit analysis, Ehrlich constructed an economic model of analysis based on two propositions about murder and other crimes against persons.

The first proposition stated that murder and other crimes against persons are committed largely as a result of hate, jealousy, and other interpersonal conflicts involving pecuniary and nonpecuniary motives or as a byproduct of crimes against property.

The second proposition stated that one's propensity to perpetrate such crimes is influenced by the prospective gains and losses associated with their commission.

Applying his economic model and a parade of statistical methods, Ehrlich analyzed aggregate crime data regarding murder and capital punishment and concluded that "law enforcement activities in general and executions in particular do exert a deterrent effect on acts of murder" (Ehrlich 1975, p. 416).

In a study conducted by the economics department at the University of Colorado, researchers reported that they found a statistically significant relationship between executions, pardons, and homicide rates. Specifically, they concluded that every execution prevents five or six additional homicides. Conversely, they claimed that pardons or commutations of death sentences result, statistically speaking, in the commission of 1.5–2 additional murders.

> *According to the standard economic model of crime, a rational offender would respond to perceived costs and benefits of committing crime. Capital punishment is particularly significant in this context, because it represents a very high cost for committing murder (loss of life). Thus the presence of capital punishment in a state, or the frequency with which it is used, should unequivocally deter homicide. (Mocan and Gittings 2001, p. 1)*

A third study conducted by faculty members of the economics department at Emory University examined death sentences imposed in the United States from 1977 to 1996 (nearly 6,000 cases). It compared changes in homicide rates in over 3,000 counties nationwide to the likelihood of being executed in each county. The results of this study, said its authors, suggested that capital punishment had a strong deterrent effect. Any increase in arrest, sentencing, or execution tended to reduce the murder rates. The study concluded that each execution, on average, resulted in 18 fewer murders (Dezhbakhsh, Rubin, and Shepard 2003).

In spite of the sense of certainty attached to these conclusions, not all researchers are persuaded. Richard Berk, professor of statistics at the University of California Los *Angeles and author of New Claims about Executions and General Deterrence: Déjà Vu All Over Again,* asserted that the data analysis used to support such claims was flawed, containing significant statistical errors caused by the problem of "influence," which occurs when a small and atypical fraction of the available data dominates the statistical results of a study.

After reanalyzing the data used in the Mocan/Gittings study as well as other studies, Berk found that the key explanatory variable used in these studies was the number of executions by state and year. Because most states in most years execute no one, and few states execute more than five people in any given year, the sample size was too small to draw any generalized conclusions.

The results raise serious questions about whether anything useful about the deterrent value of the death penalty can ever be learned from an observational study with the data that are likely to be available. With an intervention that is so highly skewed,

*a very small portion of the data will likely impart
significant influence on the results. (Berk 2004, p. 24)*

Perhaps the simplest and most straightforward argument used by those who assert the death penalty is not a deterrent is to compare the murder rates of states that use the death penalty with states that do not. States that prohibit the death penalty are Alaska, Connecticut, Hawaii, Illinois, Iowa, Maine, Massachusetts, Michigan, Minnesota, New Jersey, New Mexico, New York, North Dakota, Rhode Island, Vermont, West Virginia, and Wisconsin.

The following table, developed by the Death Penalty Information Center, shows the murder rates in states that permitted executions were consistently higher during the past two decades than in those that did not.

Table 1: Murder Rates

Year	States with Death Penalty	States without Death Penalty
1990	9.50	9.16
1991	9.94	9.27
1992	9.51	8.63
1993	9.69	8.81
1994	9.23	7.88
1995	8.59	6.78
1996	7.72	5.37
1997	7.09	5.00
1998	6.51	4.61
1999	5.86	4.59
2000	5.70	4.25
2001	5.87	4.25
2002	5.82	4.27
2003	5.9	4.1
2004	5.7	4.0
2005	5.8	4.0
2006	5.9	4.2
2007	5.8	4.1
2008	5.7	4.0
2009	5.2	3.9
2010	5.0	4.0
2011	4.89	4.13
2012	4.95	4.09
2013	4.72	3.88
2014	4.75	3.70
2015	5.17	4.26
2016	5.63	4.49

In the final analysis, the debate over the death penalty will continue, as will the practice itself, more as an act of revenge than a deterrent.

2. Meta Analysis

In 1967, the Commission on Law Enforcement and Administration of Justice, appointed by President Lyndon Johnson, concluded that the failure to conduct systematic research and evaluation put the criminal justice system in the embarrassing situation of being unable to know when programs were successful. As a result, the commission said, programs were repetitiously continued and/or expanded based on unproven theories. The commission referred to this process as "intuitive opportunism or goal-oriented guessing."

In 1996, nearly 30 years after the commission published its report, Congress mandated the attorney general to commission an independent comprehensive evaluation of the effectiveness of programs that had been designed and administered by state and local law enforcement agencies and communities to prevent crime and that were funded in whole or in part by federal grants. The amount allocated annually to such programs exceeded $3 billion.

After an extensive search directed by the National Institute of Justice, the University of Maryland Department of Criminology and Criminal Justice was selected to conduct the evaluation. Members of this faculty did not actually evaluate the effectiveness of each program; rather, they evaluated the methods used in more than 500 crime-prevention studies, using a rating scale to determine the degree to which the methodology used in a particular study met the accepted standards of scientific research.

Each study was given a rating from one to five. The higher the score, the more confidence the authors of the report assigned to the validity of the findings and the conclusions of a particular study. After receiving a score, each study was assigned to one of three classes: programs that worked; programs that didn't work; and programs that showed promise.

The authors of "Preventing Crime: What Works, What Doesn't, and What's Promising" divided crime prevention programs into the following seven categories (Sherman et al. 1996):

Community-based programs: programs designed and implemented by local community leaders. Examples included volunteer mentoring and gun buyback programs.

Family-based programs: programs intended to reduce the incidence of child abuse, domestic violence, and poor parenting, all factors thought to promote criminal behavior.

School-based programs: programs directed at students who demonstrated behavior indicative of early delinquency such as a lack of interest in school activities, poor academic performance, behavior problems, and poor attendance.

Labor market programs: programs targeted for individuals with a high propensity to commit crimes in areas with high unemployment.

Crime in places programs: programs designed to reduce crime where the rate of crime is high by making it more difficult to commit a crime, enhancing the possibility of being caught, and making crime less rewarding. "Places" as defined in the report were small areas reserved for a narrow range of functions, often controlled by a single owner, and separated from the surrounding area: stores, homes, apartment buildings, street corners, subway stations, airports, and buses.

Police crime prevention programs: programs designed based on one or more of the following hypotheses:

- The more police a city employs, the less crime will occur.

- The faster police respond to a crime scene, the less crime will occur.

- Random police patrols in public places result in less crime.

- Police patrols targeted at specific locations at times when crime is most often committed will prevent crime at those specific times and locations.

- The more arrests police make in response to reported crimes of all types, the less

- crime will occur.

- The more arrests police make for serious violent crimes committed by high-risk offenders, the less serious crime will occur.

- Increasing the quantity of police present in the community and improving the quality of the interaction between the police and citizens in the community will result in less crime.

- The more police can identify and minimize the causes of specific crime patterns, the less crime will occur.

Criminal-justice crime prevention programs: programs used by courts and corrections services to reduce the criminal activities of offenders who have already been convicted of a crime as opposed to those not yet involved in crime.

Of the more than 500 studies evaluated by the University of Maryland faculty, only 13 programs were found to be effective in preventing crime: three family-based programs; three school-based programs; one labor market-based program; one place-based program; two police-based programs; and three criminal justice-based programs.

- Family-based programs that worked were long-term, frequent home visits (by professional service providers skilled in the identified problem area) combined with participation in preschool events, which are shown to prevent delinquency; weekly visits to homes with infants, which have been shown to reduce child abuse and injuries; and family therapy by clinical staff for delinquent and predelinquent youth.

- School-based programs that worked included those aimed at building schools' capability to initiate and sustain innovation; programs aimed at clarifying and communicating norms about behavior, with an emphasis on positive reinforcement; and comprehensive instructional programs that focused on developing social competency and thinking skills such as self-control, decision making, problem solving, and communication.

- The only labor market-based program that was found to work was a short-term vocational training program for older male ex-offenders who were no longer involved in the criminal justice system.

- The sole crime prevention program for places that met the study's standards was the implementation of nuisance-abatement control measures directed at controlling drug dealing and related crime at private rental places.

- The two police-based prevention programs identified as working were increased police patrols at specific locations at times when crimes were most often committed and the proactive arrests of serious repeat offenders and drunk drivers.

- Criminal justice-based programs identified as successful included rehabilitation programs with particular characteristics (successful rehabilitation programs being characterized as those that use multiple treatment components with a structured focus on developing social, academic, and employment coping skills, and that use cognitive restructuring methods to change clearly identified overt and undesirable behaviors associated with the offender's criminal activities, as opposed to nondirective counseling focused on insight and self-esteem issues); prison-based therapeutic community substance abuse programs that operated as 24-hour live-in facilities within prisons; and the extended incarceration of offenders who continued to commit crimes at high rates.

3. Program-Specific Analysis

1. Substance Abuse Rehabilitation Programs

   In the past four decades, heavy emphasis has been placed on providing substance abuse treatment programs. The majority of criminals reportedly have a substance abuse problem, which suggests there is a high correlation between substance abuse and criminal behavior. The Bureau of Justice Statistics estimates that 60–83 percent of all offenders have used drugs at some time in their lives, which is twice the estimated rate of drug use by noncriminals (Mumola 1998).

   Substance abuse treatment programs use a variety of approaches including therapeutic communities, pharmacological maintenance, psychotherapy, and multimodal interventions. Pharmacological maintenance involves the long-term use of substitute drugs that replace the illicit drug or block its effects. Methadone and buprenorphine, both narcotic analgesics, are used as substitutes for heroin, morphine, codeine, and other opiate derivatives. Antabuse, a disulfiram that blocks the oxidation of alcohol in the bloodstream, is used to discourage alcohol consumption. A person taking Antabuse who ingests even a small amount of alcohol will experience nausea, vomiting, profuse sweating, an intense headache, muscle pain, and blurred vision.

   Multimodal interventions, as the name suggests, consist

of some combination of inpatient and outpatient services including medical care, vocational training, academic education, family therapy, pharmacological maintenance, group therapy, individual psychotherapy, and stress-management seminars (Office of National Drug Policy 2001).

In follow-up surveys sent to inmates who had successfully completed a substance abuse treatment program and those who had not, data collected by the Federal Bureau of Prisons indicated that an inmate who completed a substance abuse program was 9 percent less likely to be rearrested within the first six months following release than an inmate who did not complete such a program (Pelissier et al. 2001).

Although some argue this data proves the value of substance abuse programs, the data is weak and unrevealing for two reasons. The survey data provide only a snapshot view of success or failure just six months after release, which is far too soon to draw any generalized conclusions. The high rate of substance abuse by convicted criminals is only correlative evidence. Substance abuse treatment might lower the probability that a convicted criminal will reoffend, but it does not establish a cause-and-effect relationship or deter others from criminal behavior.

2. Sex Offender Rehabilitation Programs
   Sex offences provoke more debate over which approach is the best than any other type of criminal behavior, with the possible exception of murderers. From the classical school point of view, treatment for sex offenders is not only fruitless but undeserved.

To many in the general public, sex offenders are less than human, primarily because the victims are most often children or women. Even other criminals look down on sex offenders. In a prison environment, sex offenders are often ostracized, assaulted, or even killed by other inmates. Classical-school sanctions for sex offenses include castration, a life term in prison without the possibility of parole, and execution.

At the opposite end of the spectrum is the positivist school view. Although there is general consensus among positivist thinkers that punishment is not an effective sanction, there is disagreement over what causes a person to commit a sexual offense and how best to treat the problem.

The majority view seems to be that the cause of criminal sexual behavior is psychological in origin and that the most appropriate sanction is therapeutic intervention: psychotherapy, cognitive therapy, aversion therapy, or a combination of the three (Farkas and Stichman 2002; Winick and LaFond 2003; Rice and Harris 2003; Morse 2003).

Data collected by investigators examining recidivism rates for sex offenders suggest that treatment can lower the probability of an offender committing another sex offense upon release from confinement. The results of a meta-analysis completed in 1998 by Hanson and Bussiere indicated that 81 percent of the rapists and 87 percent of the child molesters involved in the sixty-one follow-up studies analyzed remained arrest- and/or conviction-free for a new sex offense after four to five years.

In November 2003, the US Bureau of Justice Statistics released the results of a recidivism study involving 9,691 sex offenders released in 1994 from prisons in Arizona, Maryland, North Carolina, California, Michigan, Ohio, Delaware, Minnesota, Oregon, Florida, New Jersey, Texas, Illinois, New York, and Virginia. The study supported the findings of Hanson and Bussiere. The BOJ study found that within three years of release from prison, only 3.5 individuals were convicted of a new sex offense.

Generalizations based on the data analyzed by these investigators should be made with extreme caution for two reasons: the methods used in the studies lacked uniformity, and the length of time used to measure success was short.

It should also be noted that the studies showed that a significant number of sex offenders were rearrested or reconvicted of nonsexual crimes. Investigators found that nearly 37 percent of the child molesters and over 46 percent of the rapists went on to commit a nonsexual crime; 24 percent were convicted of a new crime other than a sex offense, and 38.6 percent were returned to prison either because they committed a new crime or because they violated a condition of their parole (Hanson and Bussiere 1998; Langan and Schmitt 2003).

3. Academic Education and Vocational Training Rehabilitation Programs
According to a report published by the Bureau of Justice Statistics in January 2003, an estimated 40 percent of state prison inmates, 27 percent of federal prison inmates, and 47 percent of local jail inmates for the

years 1989 through 1997 did not have a high school diploma or GED (Harlow 2003).

The US Department of Education periodically conducts a national survey to determine the literacy proficiencies of both the general population and the prison population. The results of the last survey, conducted in 2002, indicated that the average literacy proficiency of the prison population was substantially lower than that of the general population.

Advocates for academic education and vocational training argue that providing criminals with academic education to enhance their literacy and ensure that they are vocationally trained before release from prison will lower recidivism rates, because the offender will be better prepared to secure and maintain gainful employment (MacCormick 1931; Harer 1995).

Unfortunately, none of the research conducted to date supports or refutes this argument. Stefan *LoBuglio, author of Time to Reframe Politics and Practices in* Correctional Education, says that for the past half century, researchers have attempted—in literally thousands of studies—to find statistically significant and causal connections between treatment programming and recidivism, and they have been unsuccessful.

LoBuglio attributes these failures to poorly and inadequately designed education programs and flawed research methods. The majority of studies were retrospective in nature, said LoBuglio: researchers examined programs that had occurred in the past and had no control over what data were collected.

Because many studies were conducted by the agencies administering the programs, there was also an inherent bias in favor of positive findings. Most studies failed to consider the fact that educational programs may have attracted inmates who were more disposed to low recidivism rates. It is difficult for researchers to separate the effect of correctional education programs on recidivism rate reduction when more motivated and better prepared inmates self-select into programs (LoBuglio 2001; Wilson, Gallagher, and McKenzie 2000).

4. Spiritual Education Programs
    Among those who advocate for rehabilitation, some assert that spiritual education—in the form of Bible instruction and spiritual education and training—can effectively reduce criminal behavior.

    CRIMINON (criminon.org), a program developed by L. Ron Hubbard (founder of the Church of Scientology) and Prison Fellowship (prisonfellowship.org), a religious ministry founded by Charles Colson, are examples of religious-based rehabilitation programs.

    CRIMINON claims in its promotional literature that its program "eliminates any mystery about the sources of crime and demonstrates that crime has an exact cause—loss of self-respect—which can be addressed and resolved."

    Prison Fellowship's prognostications for success are less bold than those of CRIMINON. Colson was a former aide to President Richard Nixon and an ex-convict. He served a short prison term for his role in the burglary of the Watergate Hotel, which led to Nixon resigning in order to avoid impeachment.

Independent researchers from Lamar, Duke, and Morehead State Universities statistically analyzed data collected by the Prison Fellowship on 201 male inmates from four prisons who participated in its program while incarcerated and 201 inmates who did not participate. The researchers found no overall difference in recidivism between the groups.

However, the researchers concluded that inmates who participated in high-level Prison Fellowship-sponsored Bible studies while incarcerated were significantly less likely than nonparticipants—or than low- to medium-level participants—to be arrested during the first year following their release from prison. The researchers defined high-level participation as attendance at 10 or more Bible studies during a one-year period (Johnson, Larson, and Pitts 1997).

5. Work Rehabilitation Programs

Most prison systems in the United States require able-bodied inmates to work. Virtually all prisons and jails use inmate labor in the operation of the facility because it reduces operating costs and keeps prisoners constructively occupied.

Oregon is the only state in America, and perhaps the only government entity in the world, that has a constitutional provision requiring inmates to work. In November 1994, Oregon voters approved the Prison

Reform and Inmate Work Act (Measure 17). The act amended the state constitution by mandating the following:

All inmates of state corrections institutions shall be actively engaged full-time in work or on-the-job training." Full-time is defined in the Oregon State Constitution as "the equivalent of at least forty hours per seven-day week.

Education may be provided to inmates as part of work or on-the-job training, as long as each inmate is engaged at least half of the time in hands-on training or work activity. Inmates who are deemed by corrections officials to be physically or mentally disabled, too dangerous to society, or chemically dependent to the point they are unable to participate, may be exempt from work programs.

Prisoners who are exempt because of chemical dependency must participate in appropriate drug or alcohol treatment, but prisoners who are deemed physically or mentally disabled or too dangerous are not required to participate in treatment programs.

The Oregon State Constitution now declares that "Prison work programs shall be designed and carried out so as to achieve net cost savings in maintaining government operations or so as to achieve a net profit in private-sector activities," and further specifies that "Any compensation earned [by a prisoner] (and compensation is not mandatory) shall only be used for: (a) reimbursement of all or a portion of the inmate's rehabilitation, housing, health care, and living costs;

(b) restitution or compensation to victims of the particular inmate's crime; (c) restitution or compensation to the victims of crime generally through a fund designed for this purpose; (d) financial support for immediate family of the inmate outside the corrections institution; and (e) payment of fines, court costs and applicable taxes."

None of the money earned by the prison may be spent or saved at the discretion of the prisoner. (Oregon State Constitution, Article 1, Section 41)

By amending its constitution to require that inmates work 40 hours per week, Oregon voters—inadvertently and probably unknowingly—created a unique class of citizens whose members are guaranteed jobs. This assurance is not granted to law-abiding citizens in Oregon.

Work programs are often publicized and justified as being rehabilitative, ostensibly by teaching inmates good work habits, interpersonal skills, and new work skills and by enhancing their self-esteem. Although hardly anyone would oppose requiring inmates to work, there is no evidence to support the idea that requiring them to work while incarcerated reduces the probability of their reoffending upon release (Wilson, Gallagher, and MacKenzie 2000).

John Alcock, author of Animal Behavior: An Evolutionary Approach and the Triumph of Sociobiology (2003), says that when the public learns that sociobiologists have been able to make good evolutionary sense of the attributes of hyenas, cowbirds, blue-footed boobies, and red-back spiders, perhaps they will be receptive to the possibility that sociobiologists have something important to say about humans as well.

The public's interest in what sociobiology has to say about human beings—if the public ever learns about sociobiology—will not be dependent, as Alcock asserts, on what sociobiology knows about hyenas, birds, spiders, and the like. The public will be interested in sociobiology only if what sociobiology has to say helps to solve the mystery of criminal behavior and eliminates the pain and suffering associated with it.

The public doesn't care whether criminal behavior is a product of a gene or a spandrel. The public doesn't care whether criminal behavior stems from a combination of a gene and a spandrel. The public doesn't care whether social circumstances, psychological trauma, a brain disorder, dietary or vitamin deficiencies, or chemical imbalances cause criminal behavior.

The public didn't care about the theory or science that led to Jonas Salk's development of a vaccine to prevent polio, and the public won't care about the science that leads to a cure for criminal behavior. What is of interest to the public is the result. Will the result prevent someone from become a criminal?

Discussion and debate are essential to the problem solving process, but the argument in the academic world over what causes criminal behavior and how to prevent it seems to be driven more by egotistical one-upmanship and a need for notoriety than by a need to find an answer regardless of who gets the credit.

The public is not interested in or impressed with the intellectual arguments of scholars, particularly when their objective seems to be proving one another wrong rather than collaboratively working toward a solution to a common problem. This kind of argument may satisfy, amuse, and motivate academicians to publish and achieve tenure, but the public could not care less.

4. Logic Analysis

Undoubtedly the least scientific method used to measure the effectiveness of corrections programs is logic analysis, a process based on logic and used to test the plausibility of a program or theory. The method is nonetheless revealing.

We know from the work of B. F. Skinner and others that for punishment to be effective in any setting as a behavior modifier, it must be applied swiftly in response to the behavior targeted for change, and it must be applied with certainty and consistency.

The reality is that most criminals are never caught. According to data collected in 2016 by the US Criminal Justice Information Division, 54.4 percent of all violent crimes went unsolved, and nearly 79.6 percent of all property crimes were never solved, which eliminates any possibility of consistency or certainty.

As far as swiftness is concerned, that too is highly unlikely. The American system of justice is by design a deliberate and methodical process, operated on the presumption an accused person is innocent until proven guilty. On average, it takes about six months from arrest to sentencing (Durose and Langan 2004).

If the amount of time before punishment is imposed is measured by the period from the moment a person, regardless of age, first demonstrates criminal behavior until some form of punishment is administered, the criminal justice system is even slower and equally less certain.

The typical response to criminal behavior in a youthful offender is counseling. If counseling proves ineffective and the individual continues to display chronic criminal tendencies, he or she is sent to a training school or reformatory—not as punishment but to be retrained and reformed. It is not until the offender reaches the chronological age of adulthood or is remanded to adult court because of a crime's severity that punishment is imposed as a sanction.

Although some argue the threat of punishment will deter an individual from becoming a criminal and might convince an individual not to commit further criminal acts, the same cannot be said for rehabilitation. Rehabilitation will benefit only individuals who have already committed a crime and been caught, convicted, and sentenced. The promise of rehabilitation will not deter an individual who has not yet committed a crime.

Some have the perception that the effectiveness of rehabilitation programs in prison would be significantly enhanced if prisons operated on the principles of a therapeutic community. Admission to a therapeutic community is typically voluntary, as is the decision to leave. This is not the case in a prison. People are placed in prison involuntarily and might be killed if they attempt to leave before they are authorized to do so.

The population of a therapeutic community is kept small (usually between 15 and 30) to promote interpersonal relationships between staff and residents and among the residents themselves.

     THOMAS TOOMBS, PhD

Prisons are designed to hold large numbers of people (the population of a prison can range from 100 to 3,000). The large size of the population is hardly conducive to forming supportive and mutually beneficial relationships among the prisoners or between the prisoners and those who watch over them.

In a true therapeutic community, there is no difference in status between staff and residents; they are all considered members of a family. Residents of a therapeutic community share in developing rules of conduct. They participate in imposing discipline when rules are broken and granting rewards for good conduct.

In a prison, fraternization between inmates and staff is by rule, prohibited. Employees who violate this rule are subject to discipline, up to and including termination. Staff develop the rules of conduct, imposes discipline when rules are broken, and grant rewards for good conduct.

Peer pressure is considered one of the strongest motivators to promote behavior change in a therapeutic community, and it is encouraged. Residents participate in making job assignments, granting promotions, and awarding other community privileges. Preservation of individual identity is promoted by allowing residents to wear civilian clothing of their own choice.

Given the types of behavior that most criminals manifest, it is illogical to think that confining hundreds—sometimes thousands—in the limited confines of a prison would be a therapeutic experience. The environment in a prison lends itself to reinforcing criminal values more than to diminishing them.

Rehabilitating criminal behavior starts in prison but continues long after a criminal is released, and myriad factors can negatively influence the rehabilitation process. Anyone who believes that criminals will be reformed or rehabilitated during their confinement will be disappointed with the results. The letter below was written by a former inmate, and although laced with sarcasm, it is indicative of what many criminals think.

    THOMAS TOOMBS, PhD

LESSON 4:
Efforts to Reform Prisons Should Be Abandoned in Favor of Efforts to Develop High-Tech Alternatives

Efforts to Reform Prisons Should Be Abandoned in Favor of Efforts to Develop High-Tech Alternatives

alls for prison reform have been heralded since prisons were introduced in the American colonies in the 1600s. The reasons for reform have maintained similar themes: to free those imprisoned for crimes that discriminate against certain classes of people, to improve living conditions by ensuring prisoners are provided fresh water, food, and health care, and to provide opportunity and resources for prisoners to cleanse the soul and improve the mind.

Sponsors of reform efforts have also remained relatively constant. They include influential religious leaders and groups, significant elected and appointed government officials, special interest lobbying groups, and professional organizations.

Among the early advocates for reform was a Quaker organization called the Philadelphia Society for Alleviating the Miseries of Public Prisons. Prominent people including Thomas Jefferson, Lewis Dwight, William Penn, de Tocqueville, and Dorothea Dix also advanced calls for prison reform. Recent calls for reform have come from former

President Barack Obama, Supreme Court Justice Anthony Kennedy, the American Bar Association (ABA), The Center for Prison Reform, and The MacArthur Foundation.

A proposal put forth in 2003 by the ABA—in response to a challenge from US Supreme Court Justice Anthony M. Kennedy—offered a contemporary example for prison reform. In a speech at the ABA annual meeting, Justice Kennedy chastised the legal profession for focusing too much on the process of determining guilt and innocence and paying too little attention to what happens after a prisoner is put away.

In addition to being troubled by the large number of people sent to prison, Kennedy expressed concern for the disproportionate impact of incarceration on minorities, the cost and length of incarceration, sentencing guidelines and mandatory minimum sentences, the importance of judicial discretion in sentencing, the atrophy of the pardon power, the dehumanizing experience of prison, and the importance of rehabilitation as a punishment goal.

In Kennedy's view, the resources of the criminal justice system are misspent, its punishments are too severe, and its sentences are too long. He challenged the ABA to renew public discussion about the prison system (Cohen 1995).

In response to this challenge, the ABA appointed a commission to study Kennedy's concerns. In August 2004, this commission issued a report of its findings in the form of five resolutions:

Resolution #1: The American Bar Association urges states, territories, and the federal government to ensure that prisoners are effectively supervised in safe, secure environments; that correctional staff are properly trained and supervised; and that allegations of mistreatment are promptly investigated and are dealt with swiftly and appropriately.

Resolution #2: The American Bar Association urges states, territories, and the federal government to prepare prisoners for release back into the community by implementing policies and programs that from the beginning of incarceration provide appropriate programming, including substance-abuse treatment, educational and job training opportunities, and mental-health counseling and services; and encourage prisoner participation by giving credit toward satisfaction of sentences for successful completion of such programs.

Resolution #3: The American Bar Association urges states, territories, and the federal government to assist prisoners who have been released into the community by implementing policies and programs that establish community partnerships that include corrections, police, prosecutors, and community representatives committed to promoting successful reentry into the community and that measure their performance by the overall success of reentry; and assist prisoners returning to the community with transitional housing, job-placement assistance, and substance-abuse avoidance.

Resolution #4: The American Bar Association urges states, territories, and the federal government, in order to remove unwarranted legal barriers to reentry, to identify collateral sanctions imposed upon conviction and discretionary disqualification of convicted persons from other generally available opportunities and benefits; limit collateral sanctions to those that are specifically warranted by the conduct underlying the conviction, and prohibit those that unreasonably infringe on fundamental rights or frustrate successful reentry; and limit situations in which a convicted person may be disqualified from otherwise available benefits and opportunities, including employment, to the greatest extent consistent with public safety.

Resolution #5: The American Bar Association urges law schools to establish reentry clinics in which students assist individuals who have been imprisoned and are seeking to reestablish themselves in the community to regain legal rights or remove collateral disabilities. (American Bar Association 2004)

The most recent action to reform prisons was the First Step Act, a bipartisan bill, signed into law by President Trump in 2018, intended to increase programs designed to reduce recidivism and modify sentencing laws that allowed judges to impose extended prison terms that inflated prisoner population in federal prisons, which was a cost saving provision, not a reformation provision.

Justice Kennedy's concerns the ABA's resolutions and issues addressed in the First Step Act represent a reinvention of vintage views advanced by earlier reformers. Kennedy's view of prisons and the authors of the First Step Act is predicated on the unproven theory that academic education, job training, and guidance counseling in prison—followed by equal employment opportunity in the community after release—will stop criminals from reoffending.

Past efforts to reform prisons, based on the same or similar theoretical ideas espoused by Kennedy, the ABA, and those who crafted the First Step Act provide no new insight into what causes criminal behavior or how to prevent it. It is unlikely that renewed efforts to reform prisons—based on these same ideas—will do any better.

Over the years, the design and structure of prisons have been modified. Buildings have replaced stockades, and fences have replaced walls. Cellblocks are now called "pods." The words "prison" and "penitentiary" have been dropped in favor of "correctional center," "reformatory," or "correctional institution." Even the label placed on occupants has changed from "convict" to "prisoner," "inmate," "resident," or even "client."

Tom Gaddis, author of *The Birdman of Alcatraz*, referred to this word game as a "semantic mantel." By this, he meant that labels for programs, policies, and practices in corrections were changed to reflect progress, enlightenment, and improvement, when in reality no substantive change had occurred. No matter what its design or structure, no matter what its name, and no matter what its occupants are called, a prison is a prison.

While other fields and disciplines are developing new ways of using high-tech knowledge to improve practices, the field of corrections is not. Consider technologies that have increased the effectiveness of endeavors in other fields: laser surgery, computerized x-rays, arthroscopic surgery, robotic assembly, computerized drafting, and laser-guided weapons systems.

In contrast to medical services, manufacturing, and military defense, America's corrections system continues to rely almost exclusively on traditional probation programs and some form of a prison to control criminals. Infrared, microwave, and fiber-optic technologies are used to improve prison perimeter control systems; computers are sometimes used to automate inmate count; and robotic sentries are available (although not heavily used). In contrast to other fields, the development and application of new technologies in corrections is almost nonexistent.

One form of new technology that holds great potential for improving corrections ability to monitor and control the whereabouts of criminal offenders in the community is surgically implanted transponders monitored by satellites. Perhaps the technology could be used as a true alternative to prison for many types of criminal offenders, both adult and juvenile who are currently imprisoned.

A system of satellites capable of tracking mobile transponders is already in orbit around the earth. The system is used extensively by the U.S. military, the transportation industry, and hikers, hunters, and other outdoor enthusiasts. A shoe is being developed for Alzheimer patients that will make it easier for caretakers to instantly identify the patient's whereabouts. The use of implanted microchips, however, is currently limited to exotic animals and to assist in their recovery if stolen.

Transponders in a bracelet or anklet are widely used in the United States as well as other countries. Such devices help pinpoint the location of an offender, as long as the anklet or bracelet is not removed. If the anklet or bracelet is removed, however, it is of no use helping to locate the offender.

Requiring sex offenders, rapists, or other predatory criminals to register with local law enforcement, and to publicize their addresses to the community, serves no useful purpose if those accountable for monitoring and controlling the whereabouts of the offender have no way of knowing the offender's location. We may know sooner, when an anklet or bracelet is removed that an offender has escaped, but the removal does not reveal the more important information; where has the offender gone.

To know their location at any given moment requires a new approach such as surgically implanted transponders. Unlike an electronic anklet or bracelet, a surgically implanted transponder could not be easily removed or deactivated.

The transponder could be monitored by a satellite surveillance system and alert authorities immediately if an offender leaves an authorized area or enters an unauthorized area without permission, and it would allow authorities to track and apprehend the offender.

Such a system could be used to gain better control over criminals on probation or parole. It could also be used to allow criminals who pose a low risk to harm others and are currently confined in prison to be safely monitored and controlled in the community.

Comparatively speaking, the cost of monitoring and controlling criminals using surgical implants and satellite surveillance systems would be significantly less than the existing prison system.

In October 2004, the US Food and Drug Administration approved the use of the first radio frequency identification (RFID) chip for humans. It was developed by Digital Angel Corporation. The Verichip is about the size of a grain of rice; once inserted, it is undetectable by the human eye. It can be inserted by syringe under the skin for $150 to $200.

A number of private sector companies have formed to provide tracking services and the cost for tracking criminals outfitted with an electronic anklet or bracelet has been advertised for as low as $8.75 per day, which should not be appreciably different for tracking a surgically implanted transponder.

In addition to replacing an antiquated methodology and improving the ability to monitor and control convicted criminals, the use of surgically implanted transponders has the potential to significantly reduce the cost of correctional services.

As radical as it may sound, efforts to reform prisons should be abandoned in favor of efforts to replace them. Prisons represent an antiquated, expensive concept. Their goal is to deter criminal behavior through punishment, rehabilitation or both.

The results of the studies discussed and cited previously, no matter how accurately or inaccurately the study was designed, all suggest prisons do not effectively deter criminal behavior no matter what the prison's operating philosophy. Continuing efforts to reform prisons only perpetuate their existence and obstruct discoveries of what causes criminal behavior and how to prevent it; and consume astronomical amounts of money that could be better used to fund other social programs like education and health care.

Appendix

I started my first job in November 1964 as a psychometrician at the Penitentiary. In February 1966, I received a letter from Uncle Sam directing me to report for military duty.

Upon discharge from the military in February 1968, I returned to work at the penitentiary as a correctional counselor. I was enrolled in a two-week reorientation program and had just completed the first week when a riot broke out.

During the riot, nine convicts and a correctional lieutenant in charge of the library and hobby shop, Lieutenant Ed Ben, were locked in the hobby shop on the third floor of the Intermediate Building, which was engulfed in flames on the building's first two floors.

The group made numerous attempts to escape from the hobby shop down the stairwell of the building, but entering the stairwell was like entering a chimney. The group was driven back into the hobby shop by smoke and heat from the fires.

In desperation, the inmates, under Lt. Ben's direction, began trying to cut the bars out of one window which overlooked a roof area one floor below that was not engulfed in fire, using a jeweler's saw inmates used to make jewelry that they sold in a gift shop outside the prison walls.

The bars were heat-treated steel made especially for jails and prisons, which the manufacture guaranteed could not be cut by any means. The jeweler's saw broke in short order. Lt. Ben said at that point he remembered that when he was a boy, an uncle told him a saw blade lost its cutting ability from heat generated by friction, not from the type of material being sawed.

Chagrined but still determined, the group turned to using a handheld wood saw, cooling the blade with water obtained through a hose that inmates on the ground outside the window delivered to them.

Amazingly, after 90 minutes, they were able to cut through and remove two bars, creating an opening that was approximately 9" high and 18" wide. To everyone's surprise and disbelief, all nine inmates and Lt. Ben escaped through that small opening and avoided being burned alive in the raging fire that was migrating up toward the library and hobby shop.

The following photographs, taken by Grant Yoder, Admission and Discharge Officer, show Lt. Ben surveying the opening through which he and the nine inmates escaped and the fire damage to the library and hobby shop, the area from which they escaped.

Lt. Ben

     THOMAS TOOMBS, PhD

The Library

The Hobby Shop

After the riot, Lt. Ben prepared the following report that provided a chronological account of what he perceived transpired in the libraries and hobby shop during the riot. He also asked the inmates who were confined with him if they would write down what they remembered from the experience. The personal accounts of what five of the nine inmates recalled from that horrifying experience are included. The accounts have been transcribed from their original handwritten format into typewritten format, but no other changes have been made. They are presented exactly as written.

Personal Account of 1968 Oregon State Penitary Riot

My name is Edmond A. Ben. I was born December 25, 1927. I am presently a lieutenant at the Oregon State Penitentiary. I was employed by the state of Oregon as a correctional officer October 20, 1952 (20 October 52). The following is a chronological report of an event that transpired at the Oregon State Penitentiary on Saturday, 9 March 1968.

On this date I was assigned as the hobby shop supervisor-librarian and also the legal library supervisor. I had been assigned to this post in December 1963 and since that date filled this post at Oregon State Penitentiary.

On this particular date, 9 March 68 I was preparing to depart from my post at approximately 4:05 p.m. I had completed searching the inmate workers in the hobby shop and excused them from the hobby shop to return to their cell assignments.

All of the inmates had departed from the library section as well as the legal library section with the exception of inmates Chesley, Estabrook, and Wolfe. Inmate Chesley worked for me as a typist, inmate Estabrook was a cellmate of inmate Chesley and periodically did extra work for me in the library. Inmate Wolfe had been assigned to the hobby shop and was late departing from the library on this particular date. I had completed securing all the locks in the library and in the hobby shop and was in the process of departing with the three inmates when inmate Brown returned to the library section. Inmate Brown had been assigned in the hobby shop as a hobby shop worker and just a few moments prior had been released from the hobby shop with the rest of the hobby shop crew. Inmate Brown stated, "Lieutenant, do not leave. They are knocking officers in the head down in the control room." The hobby shop and library are located on the third floor of the intermediate building, the control room being the ground floor, the classification department being on the second floor, and the library and hobby shop on the third floor, the education department being on the top floor being fourth floor.

I started for the front door of the library and inmate Brown repeated, "Don't leave Lieutenant." I informed him I was going to lock the hallway door leading from the stairway. When I arrived at the hallway door to secure the lock inmates Miller, Thompson, Pullen, Williams and Cornell, all hobby shop workers, had returned to the library floor. These inmates came through the hallway door into the library floor.

I asked them what was going on and they stated that there was a ruckus in the control room area and that it was safer for me not to depart at this time. I thereupon instructed the nine inmates to return inside the library and I secured the hallway door with padlock that normally hangs on the door. I seated the nine inmates around the library table in an area where they could not be observed from the entrance door, my plan being to stand by the door and attempt to keep anyone from entering the library and hobby shop section. My reasoning being that anyone entering that floor would have to reach through the barred section in order to gain access to the padlock that I had secured to this gate. I had gone to the restroom area and picked up a toilet brush and also armed myself with a knife from bindery section and I was very certain that I could hold off anyone trying to enter this section of the penitentiary.

I called the reception desk; I do not remember the name of the officer answering the telephone. I informed that I was the opinion that we had lost control of the control room area to the inmates and I asked him if he was aware of this situation. He told me that he was and I asked him if assistance had been called. He told me he could not locate anyone. I asked him if he had called the state police and if he had not then he should call the state police immediately. Shortly thereafter I called the reception desk again and Mr. Myers, the canteen manager, answered the phone. I informed Mr. Myers that I was still in the library with nine inmates and would remain in that area.

I remained in the library section approximately one hour. I noticed that the room had begun to fill with quite an amount of smoke. It appeared that the greatest amount of smoke was coming from the deputy warden custody office. There were only two windows leading into the library area, one was directly over the deputy warden custody office and one between E block and chapel area.

The smoke seemed to be filtering up through the floor. Also looking out through the windows of the hobby shop, I could see quite an amount of smoke coming from the shop area and I assumed at that time that the shop area had also been ignited. After the library filled with smoke I could see that the hobby shop area was still quite clear; you could see there wasn't near the amount of smoke in the hobby shop as we were experiencing in the library. I returned to the phone again and attempted to phone the reception desk, but that the phone was not operating.

Approximately 15 to 20 minutes after this whole thing started I could hear what appeared to me to be tear gas grenades being set off or tear gas shells being set off in the cell blocks. I assured the inmates with me that our stay in the library would be a short one because at that time I was fairly certain in my mind that our riot squad had entered the control room area and it was in the process of clearing the cell blocks. I later found that no such action was taken and it began to prey on my mind as to why no one was coming up to the library area to remove us.

Shortly after this whole mess started, I could hear inmates going through the cell block areas breaking glass, screaming, hollering, and all the normal things that seem to go on during this type of operation. I had no idea at first of the magnitude of this disturbance. I thought that our riot squad would be in to quell the disturbance, but after time went on, I got to wondering exactly what our situation was. I finally removed the inmates from the library area to the hobby shop area. I placed inmate Estabrook in a position in the hobby shop where he could observe the padlock I had secured the hallway gate with so he could alert me in the event that someone attempted to remove the lock. We stayed in the hobby shop area approximately 20 minutes and inmate Estabrook called me and said "Lieutenant, I cannot see the lock any longer." I assumed at that time that someone had removed the lock and upon checking I could see that he meant the smoke was so thick in the hallway that it was impossible to see the lock because of the smoke, not because someone had removed it. The lock was approximately 10 feet from his position and I would say about 3 feet from the floor, so the smoke at that time was thick enough that inmate Estabrook could not see it

Prior to this time the inmates had told me that they would stay with me in the library and hobby shop area for as long as I wanted to stay. They would not depart; they would stay in that section for as long as I decided that we should remain in that section. After the smoke had gained the intensity it had, I decided it was time for me to leave the area and the

        THOMAS TOOMBS, PhD

inmates with me, that it was no longer possible for us to remain in the area without suffocating. So inmate Miller and I went to the stairway to check it for rioting convicts and sure that our departure would be somewhat safe to take the other inmates down the stairway. When we arrived on the stairway we discovered that the smoke and the heat coming up the stairwell, well, it was literally unbearable. It drove us back up the stairway into the hobby shop. Inmate Miller tried it one more time and I tried it one more time, The smoke kept getting thicker and thicker; as a matter of fact it got so thick that the last time that I tried to go down the stairway I passed within a foot of Miller standing in the doorway of the hobby shop and he did not see me. The door blew shut and inmate Miller thought that I was trapped on the stairway because the locking device on the door would automatically lock when the door was shut. Inmate Miller took a metal stool and threw it through the window in the attempt to go out in the stairway to find me. When I heard the breaking glass I hollered at him because I had passed directly by him and gone to the window on the east side of the hobby shop. The door was on the west side of the hobby shop.

At this time, inmate Miller and I searched through the hobby shop in the attempt to locate some sort of tools to break through the bars on the east side of the hobby shop. I had come to the conclusion that our only means of escape from this burning build-ing was either down through the stairway which proved to be impossible by three different attempts by inmate Miller and myself or out through the bars. In our search we came up with one jeweler saw and two propane blow torches. Inmate Miller attempted to cut the bars with his jeweler saw. At the first swipe of the bars the blade broke. These blades are small, about hair thin, and the blade broke immediately. So inmate Miller lit up two propane torches and placed them on the bottom of one of the bars in an attempt to take the temper out of the bar. I could see that the two torches were not doing any type of heating on the bars. As a matter of fact, it didn't even appear to me that it was even burning the paint from the bars let alone take the temper out of the bars.

In one last attempt I noticed we had two wood saws, one being a 12 point finishing saw and the other a rip saw; both made by the Henry Diston Company. I picked up the finishing saw and went to the bars with it and started to saw the bars. Inmate Miller asked me what I was trying to do because he thought I had gone off my rocker I guess, using a wood saw on metal bars. However, I told him take a port in a storm, it was either cut the bars or we were gone. So I started to use the saw on the bars and he told me to stop and I asked why. He said that the saw is cutting the bar and we don't want to turn the teeth over on the saw. I informed him that we had a water hose there and water on the saw so that the saw blade would not get too hot and turn the teeth over. As long as I kept the saw cool it would cut through the bars.

Inmate Brown located a hand saw in his hobby shop cabinet and brought it to the barred section where I was sawing and proceeded to use his saw on one side of the bar while I sawed on the other. Just prior to our attempt to saw the bars out with the hand saw a group of inmates appeared outside the window with a fire hose. They sprayed the hobby shop with water and subsequently pushed the end of the fire hose through the window into the hobby shop for us to use. The hose reached approximately five to six feet into the hobby shop area itself. Looking directly below us toward the commissary gate area the site of the milling, rioting convicts was all around; looking to the east, the furniture factory, plumbing shop, carpenter shop, vocational training section, and all the physical plant. T area seemed to be a burning inferno.

Inmates Burton, Griffin, Cameron and Quayle were on the outside of the window attempting to help us break out from the hobby shop. Inmate Quayle was the first one I noticed and had the fire hose I spoke of. He brought the hose up to us and kept hosing the area down and finally ended up pushing the hose into the hobby shop to us. Inmates Burton, Griffin and Cameron came up when we started to saw the bars out and one of the three I believe showed up there with a sledge hammer so it wasn't necessary to saw clear threw the bars. We sawed practically all the way through the top of both bars that we removed and sawed part way through the bottom of the bars and struck the bars with the sledge hammer and knocked them out. After we got these bars out, inmates pushed me out through the bars first. Inmate Burton, I believe it was, told me to stand behind him so the other inmates outside the area would not recognize me. When we made our departure from the hobby shop we came out on top of the ramp leading from the control room to the dining room. From there it was a drop two floors down to the ground floor level.

Before we got these bars sawed out, before we discovered we could saw the bars with a hand saw, wood-type saw, we hollered down to the inmates asking them where the fire trucks were and they stated the fire trucks the fire trucks would not come inside because hostages were being held down by the gate where the fire trucks would normally come in. We attempted to get some of the inmates to bring us a cutting torch so that we could cut the bars and they informed us that no cutting torch was available. However inmate Griffin, one of the inmates that helped us finally remove the bars, spotted Captain Lucas to get us a cutting torch for him from the shop areas that was not being destroyed by fire. He was not successful. He was not successful in getting a cutting torch to bring back to the hobby shop so we were without a cutting torch to remove any of the bars.

After I finally crawled through the bars and stood behind Burton on this roofed area, two or three other inmates came out through the bars. Below this catwalk we have a cement block wall and I could readily see that if I dropped down on one side of the wall that the rioting inmates could not see me. The only obstruction standing between me and the wall and the safety of fellow officers with loaded weapons was on chain-link fence. I decided that I would make my

   THOMAS TOOMBS, PhD

way down a drain pipe to ground level and head for the north wall. I was fairly certain that once the inmates had departed from the hobby shop they could drop down the other side of the walled section. I figured that they could go back down into the control room area and make their way back to their cell blocks. I did not at this time that the other inmates, the rioting inmates, were in the process of burning the entire control room area and tearing up all the cell blocks to the extent they were torn up.

I worked my way to the chain-link fence that separates the commissary from D block on the south end. I took my white handkerchief in my pocket and waved it through the gate trying to gain the attention of the tower officer. I could not get the tower officer to acknowledge that he saw me. I could not gain any recognition from him and was uncertain as to whether I should try to crawl the fence and take my chance of getting shot off the fence or to stay where I was because I could see inmates on the sun porch of the hospital. I was uncertain as to their stand in this situation. I didn't know if they would start throwing stuff from the sun porch area in the attempt to stop me. So I crawled the fence, got up on top, lying on top of the barbwire and I hollered at the tower officer, I later learned it was officer Luthey and still could not get his attention. I dropped down from the fence to the grass on the outside the fence and decided if I walked directly toward the wall that someone would stop me. I did not know at this time that someone had issued orders for tower officers not to fire their weapons. But I proceeded to walk toward the wall and had only traveled a short distance when an officer appeared between 8 and 9 towers. I later learned this officer was officer Tibbles. He motioned for me to lie down in the grass- I thought that was his instructions, anyway, and at this time I lost my temper and cursed him quite violently and told him who I was and ordered him to give me clearance past tower 9 so that I could go out the gate at Turnkey. The officer at this time ran down to the 9 tower and I was thereupon granted clearance to the Turnkey area. I waited there a short time and they finally brought a key out to the gate and admitted me through the gate.

I went with Captain Lucas up into the business office. My first recollection of the business office was a mass of newspaper reporters, people with cameras, and so forth. At time I was in no mood to be photographed, no mood to be giving statements. I guess I was quite exciting at this time because I was shirtless, my clothes were badly torn. I was bleeding from the cuts not caused by damage from the inmates, but from being tangled up in barbwire, getting cut from going through the window, not from the glass but from where we had removed the bars from the window. We didn't do a real neat job, so to speak, and the bars had torn my shirt and cut me on the chest. I went with Captain Lucas and Deputy Warden Francis to the Warden's office in an attempt to gain some privacy, to explain to them my departing procedure from the hobby shop; but upon entering the Warden's office I was again confronted by a multitude of strangers with cameras, not pads, and so forth. I finally got Captain Lucas off into a

 THOMAS TOOMBS, PhD

corner and gave him a short run down on what happened and how I got out of the hobby shop. As soon as I could after that I called my home to notify my family that I was okay, that we had a little difficulty at the penitentiary, that I would be late in arriving home from work.

During the time we were attempting to break out of the hobby shop, we hollered down at the inmates below us in an attempt to relay word to the people holding the hostages to backup from the gate area so the trucks would come in to fight the fire in our area. One answer was that those guys don't give a damn; they have already killed a bunch of officers in the control room. At that time, I was quite concerned because several friends of mine were working in the control room area. It later proved that no officers were actually killed. A number were injured and it also materialized that four of my fellow officers were held hostage in the yard overnight. After we had been informed that the officers had been killed in the control room the inmates with me in the hobby shop suggested that I remove my shirt so that I would not be identified. I removed my shirt and used it in the attempt to screen out smoke and thereby make breathing a little easier.

In replaying these two tapes I noticed that on the prior tape I refer to a door that I locked in the attempt to keep other inmates from gaining access to the library and hobby shop. This should be clarified to mean the hallway gate; that is a gate from the stairway to the hallway area. This is a barred gate and not a door.

During this report various inmates are mentioned. I will now give you their names, birthdates, their crime and their sentence. These facts are typed in specific order and not identified otherwise.

1. Miller, 12-29-25, kidnapping, 25 years

2. Thompson, 2-19-14, second degree murder, life

3. Pullen, 3-25-38, burglary in a dwelling, 10 years

4. Brown, 11-28-28, rape, 12 years

5. Chesley, 7-4-35, assault and robbery being armed with a dangerous weapon and second degree murder, 2 life sentences

6. Estabrook, 7-7-42, assault with a dangerous weapon, 5 years

7. Williams, 3-23-23, murder and ex-con in possession of a firearm, life and 4 years

8. Wolfe, 11-28-38, second degree murder, life

9. Cornell, 6-12-28, 2 first degree murders, 2 life sentences

10. Burton, 5-19-42, habitual criminal, life

11. Griffin, 2-5-14, habitual criminal, 30 years

 THOMAS TOOMBS, PhD

Testimonial by Roger L. Pullen:

Unforgettable Impression
(3/9/68)

Upon entering the control center from the hobby shop at 4:10 P.M. Saturday afternoon I heard a commotion, cussing and yelling.

Stepping around the corner headed for "C" block I saw convicts running and yelling with weight bars after officers. Directly in front of "D" block an officer was down with two cons working him over with pipes. Directly to my right was a large officer with a knife against the wall. Lient., Pribble was standing in the control house door brandishing a club into his hands. It seemed to me that he was indecisive as to whether he should go to the aid of the stricken officer, or protect the room itself.

At this point I backed into the stairway thinking that I'd better warn those left upstairs and lend assistance to protecting the hobby shop and those still there.

It looked at first as though it was merely a fight, but upon seeing the knives and clubs I knew in my own mind that what I had been fearing had happened. Riot, as that's all it could be.

Upon entering the library we spread the word. At this point I was expecting the riot squad to move in and take over. There was really no apprehension on my part at this time.

An hour later I still expected that within minutes it would be over. Then without warning someone smelled smoke. Many things ran through my mind, but the main thing was that at least I had a witness that I had nothing to do with the riot.

Upon moving into the hobby shop I felt that we could protect ourselves better, as the fighting front was smaller and weapons were more available. It was extremely difficult to stay away from the windows as we all wanted to see what was happening, but at the time we didn't want to let anyone know that we were up there, thusly reminding them that the hobby shop had numerous weapons. I was not looking forward to ten of us fighting half the joint. We did hope though that we could hold them off until help arrived.

At this point most of, or at least some of us began to be concerned with Lient., Bens safety, as we witnessed the treatment, and humiliation of Lientl, Pribles through the windows of the hobby shop. He was being manhandled in front of the canteen. I never knew the man, but upon seeing the cons spit on him and the general way he was treated it shocked me. I never in my life felt lower than that moment for being a convict, or even a member of the human race for that matter. But at the same time my faith in mankind moved up a notch as I watched the way Lient., Prible took it. With everything that he was going through, he took it without a movement. I couldn't help but notice that he was a good man with reserves of courage. I can't help but feel that he knew his life was hanging on a whim of a couple of crazy, mob crazy kids.

When the smoke started getting thicker we began to think about getting out as it hadn't dawned on any of us at that time that we may be in danger of dying by fire.

     THOMAS TOOMBS, PhD

Three of tried the stairs as an escape route but Lient. Ben who was leading turned back, and I who was last in line agreed completely, as the smoke at the time was impossible.

Upon re-entering the hobby shop we grabbed what rags that were available and stuffed them under the door attempting to stop as much smoke as possible. Someone suggested that we wet rags and hold them to our face for protection. But upon opening the utility room door we were nearly floored by the smoke boiling out, as there must have been a vent from it into the library, which had been obscured by smoke for quite sometime. Anyway we wet the rags and slammed the door.

A short time later it became impossible to stay at that end of the shop, as the men were gasping for breath steadily. To me it was a desperate moment indeed, as it was at this time that I knew if we were going to get out alive, it would have to be through the barred windows. Personally I'd never given much thought to my chances of going through bars without tools.

We moved to the windows letting those cons out by the canteen know that we trapped and to get us to hell out of there. At this point Lient., Ben stood away from the windows as we didn't know what their reaction would be if they knew he was present. And from what we had observed so far it couldn't have been good. Most of the cons started yelling that "There's cons trapped in the hobby shop" and proceeded to run around in circles giving orders, unfortunately they were all chiefs and no privates. Needless to say I was rapidly becoming worried as we could barely see what we doing in the shop due to the smoke.

Finally, on con got on the roof and started spraying the fire hose up in the windows, but personally I felt that the good it did was negligible. Outside of maybe our morale, but when he hit me in the face with the full force of the water, my morale washed away with my patience.

Then Silas crawled up to the bars and yelled that he would try to round up a cutting torch, believe me, that man was never so welcome. I began to think that maybe there was a chance after all. While he was gone my hopes were high, but upon his return they again plummeted, as he stated he had talked to Captain Lucas and that he refused to allow a torch in until all the cons were moved to the yard. This we knew would never happen as a yelled comment had been made that if we died then the press would listen and maybe do something." Personally I feel that his attitude would have changed drastically if our geography locations were reversed."

A few minutes later Si sent in an eight pound sledge hammer to Bob and the Lient., but upon working on the bars it became evident that the handle was cracked and extreme care would have to be utilized in order to prevent its breaking completely.

Upon hearing this my heart started pounding rather rapidly, then to make matters worse the con holding the fire hose kept yelling that the upstairs was about to fall in due to the fire. I kept thinking of the Ohio State Prison fire that killed over three hundred inmates.

There was only room for a couple at the window to work so the rest of us scattered out along the remaining shop windows to breath.

At this point we could se nothing in the shop, not even ourselves, away from the windows. Someone came up with a jewelers saw, but to no avail as it wouldn't cut. Then a carpenters saw was tried, but it too was useless as the teeth were set to much. Finally a carpenters finish handsaw was tried and cut some, but those of us who could not tell how it was progressing. This was hard to take, as from the reactions of the men around me, as well as myself we were quite desperate. In fact when the hole was finally announced it surprised us all, or at least me.

I heard my name being called and so we started blindly along the top of the tables toward the sounds of the voices. Upon reaching the end of the tables I fell off onto the floor, (I think not very gracefully) upon grapping round I felt a leg and wall. As I rose into a standing position I saw Silas and Bob pulling someone through the hole.

Upon seeing the size of the hole I was dismayed, as it seemed impossible for anyone to pass through it., but at the same time I was determined that beings we'd made it this far everyone was going through, broken ribs or not.

Bob yelled at me to get in but before I could, I was pushed aside by one who was in a bigger hurry than I. Then he got hung up as his hips were difficult to get through. Finally I was put through and proceeded to help Si pull the rest out.

All in all, I was a very relieved individual and was happy that everyone turned out as it did. I've some doubts that we could have lasted much longer.

Testimonial by Billie M. Brown:

This a factual account of what took place in the Library and hobby shop as seen by me, Billie H. Brown.

Today I was asked to write this essay on that which took place or rather what I saw and felt during the riot. This should be an easy task because I shall never forget those hours of dread and the agonizing attempts to draw a breath of fresh cool air. I sound a bit dramatic or tend to make certain others look like heroes, it is only because that is the way it looked to me.

We were leaving the hobby shop on this fateful Saturday evening, several of the men had already gone down ahead of me. With my mind filled with thoughts of what I would do on Sunday and unsuspecting of the havoc that was to take place, and was taking place; I stepped to the door of the control center: looking up, the first that I saw was an officer standing alone in the room with blood running from his mouth, then everything hit me at once.

Men were running and screams were made all over the room. One officer was down and two men were beating on him with a third trying to kick him. Another officer ran towards the gate leading to the front of the prison, but just as he reached the gate an inmate whom, I do not know but will never forget, charged him and started to beat him.

Mr. Pribble stepped to the door of the control room slapping his hand with a piece of pipe or something. I heard an inmate call out lets get all these damn bulls. Another screamed kill the ______.

At this time I thought of Lt. Ben alone in the hobby shop except for a few other cons. All of this, that is to say from the time I reached the control room door until I thought of Lt. Ben, was bout 5 to 10 seconds time.

I turned and ran back up the stairs and told Lt. Ben that there was a riot going on down there: he said "are you kidding?" I said no I am serious. Lt. Ben then looked startled and I told him that the cons were beating the officers. He (Lt. Ben) started towards the door, I thought he was going to try and help them so I told or rather screamed at him "Ben don't go down there". He said I am going to lock this door. About this time Bob Miller and some other inmates, whom I had passed on my dash back up the stairs, come in the door. Lt Ben than locked the door and we all went to the center of the room and sat down at a word from Lt. Ben. As we sat there there were loud noises, windows being broken yells and screams and many other sounds filled the air.

Then Lt. Ben got on the phone and called somewhere, the front office I believe, then sat back and seemed to relax. I looked at him and marveled at his coolness, how could this man in the face of a riot, penned in with 9inmates that he had no way of knowing if they were friendly or unfriendly at this time, remain so cool I wondered. He walked back to us and spoke to us then went out and turned off the lights. I sure wanted a cigarette then I remembered that I had quit smoking 4 years ago.

We sat there for some time and the smoke began to pour in from down below, we kept looking for that riot squad or state police or someone else to come.

The Lt. told the ones who wanted to stay to stay and if anyone wanted to go that they could do so but no one moved. Bob Miller sat there thinking but seemingly unmoved. The others all looked a bit frightened and unsure of themselves. I was afraid as the others looked. I knew that no one was after me but knew too that anyone that would try and get Lt. Ben would set me at odds with them. I looked at all the men again to try to see how they felt. Finally, Lt. Ben said to that the others would have a hard time getting through the door. We assured or tried to assure him that no one would get through the door, that is, Bob Miller and I said this anyway.

Lt. Ben walked down to the book binding room, again I wondered at the way he used his head and seemed as if the felt that he had everything under control, which he did for we all were with him as a man, but he still didn't know this.

After a while Miller joined him in the book binding room. I sat there for a while and went to the bathroom and then Lt. Ben and Miller asked me in to the binding room with them. Miller had a hammer and they were watching the door. I got a few glasses of water because I didn't know but what the water would be cut off any time. "Where is that riot squad". At about this time an inmate named Harvy Oday came up the stairs and looked around (he later told me that he was looking for a place to get out of the mess and that the place looked deserted so he went back out, he said he wanted no part of the riot.)

The smoke began to thicken so that we couldn't see across the room and we knew that we had to get

 THOMAS TOOMBS, PhD

out of the smoke. Lt. Ben then let open the door to the shop. At this time in spite of the smoke, I felt that the one thing to fear was the inmates getting to Lt. Ben. If there was any fear of what might happen he sure didn't show it. I think he knew he was in command at this time. I made some crack about the fact I played the part of a mere person but I thought they were going to see a scared man fight. I just knew that sooner or later the rioters would think about the knives and tools in the shop and come looking for them and I knew that if they did and found Lt. Ben there would be trouble and that Miller would fight to the death and I would do no less. Damn that Ben why does he have to act as if this is a church social, doesn't he know his very life is in danger (I didn't know how close to the truth that was).

I went to my locker and got my hammer out, I felt better with it. Now the smoke is so thick that it is painful to breath. The Lt. went down the hall to try to find a place where the air was better, but I stayed in the shop. The smoke in the hall was worse. I didn't see Miller go out with him. Now the smoke was so thick I was afraid for Lt. Bens life so I called to him a couple of times. At this time Miller came back in and said that he thought the smoke was less back where Mr. Ben was so we started to hold hands (the smoke was so thick that we were afraid we would loose some one) Then Lt. Ben came in and said the smoke there was worse. We went to the windows to breath and someone with a hose was trying to get it to run water.

We watched for a while and smoke became thicker. Some time during this time I went over and closed the toilet door because smoke was really pouring in from it. I remembered that the floor was already hot through my shoes. Miller told me to close the window over the toilet door and I did. I don't know what the rest of the men were doing but most seemed to be over by the windows for air. The smoke was bad but now it became most unbearable. We knew then that we had to get out.

Mr. Ben braved the smoke and unlocked the door to the stairs but then to our dismay we found that from the classification department came so much smoke and heat that to go down the stairs was impossible. We were trapped and there seemed no escape. The smoke forced us all over to the windows in the hobby shop.

The inmate outside with the hose had got the water to running and was trying to put out the fires, he saw us and shot a stream of water at us (we thought) but he only thought we were on fire up there too and was trying to help us. Lt. Ben then asked me about a saw that I had, he said I didn't think it would cut the bars because Miller had tried to cut them with a jewelers saw and tried with a metal cutting blade in my coping saw and they wouldn't cut them.

The smoke black and oily boiled around us until we couldn't see or breath. Lt. Ben then got a hand saw and went for the bars. I called to him to stay away from the window "don't let them see you" I said not knowing that most of those who were after the officers were by this time out in the yard. He went on to the window and the man with the hose was there on the roof of the

    THOMAS TOOMBS, PhD

canteen, he asked Mr. Ben who was with him. Lt. Ben started to saw the bars with the hand saw and I ran to my locker and got my plumbers saw and joined Lt. Ben. We knew that we either had to get out fast or die.

The saws worked but seemed very slow The men on the roof sent for a sledge hammer and Billy Ogden went and got one (I think it was him) Lt. Ben, Miller and I stepped back and they used the sledge hammer outside. Bob Miller and I had tried to use torches to heat the bars to soften them but the flame lacked oxygen enough to burn hot. I put my finger in the flame and said that it wouldn't work. Our lungs were aching and I heard one man say "we can't make it the smoke is going to get us." And it seemed that way too but we had to try,

I don't why it was that just Miller, Lt. Ben and I were making an effort to get free, I guess the others felt they could do little. The hose man told someone to go for help, then a short while later he shouted, "he knocked him down, he went to get help and Capt. Lucas knocked him down."

Lt. Ben said then, "we will make it". He didn't sound to sure this time. I had the foolish thought "by golly he isn't a super man after all" but I wasn't to sure of that because he never panicked and his coolness kept things in order and I am quite sure that he saved our lives, after all I had tried to saw out with metal coping saw blade, Miller had tried with a jewelers saw and we gave it up.

It was Lt. Ben who thought of the larger hand saw and my plumbers saw. I had honestly just about given up and most of the others had too. Miller, as strong as he was, was about to the end of his strength. I guess we both grew strength from Lt. Ben.

Well the sledge work on the outside did two things. 1. broke a chip off of cement and 2. broke the handle. Lt. Ben then picked up the saw and went back to work and I, drawing strength from this picked up my saw and went back to work. Lt. Ben at the top of the bar and I at the bottom.

After an agonizingly long time we managed to cut half through the bars, then Miller took the sledge and holding the handle together put his shoulders behind the blows and soon broke the bar free. In desperation we to work on another bar with renewed vigor. We just couldn't breath as there was no air to be had and sticking our head to the bars didn't help much.

On this bar we cut only at the top, Lt. Ben first then me, I handed the saw to a man outside but it was to high for him to saw so taking the saw again I sawed until I had to get air then Miller sawed for a while and gave the saw back to Lt. Ben. This went on until the bar was half through. Miller hit with a sledge but it wouldn't break. I heard the men at the other window talking and one was saying goodbye to the other. Time was getting very short. I gave up I'm dead and I knew it but I took the saw and sawed some on the other side. Miller again hit the bar. The top broke but the bottom held. I just quit. Lt. Ben sawed more at the bottom of the bar. I'm sure I see him stagger I feel ashamed of myself for being weak and ashamed o the men that didn't help saw out (they couldn't because there just wasn't room at the window but I wasn't thinking straight and was sick).

I looked at Lt. Ben again and took the saw and sawed more and soon the bar was sawed half through. Miller looks beat and I doubt he will be able to use the hammer with force enough to bend the bar, but he taking the hammer struck it a few blows and it gave a little, and then it broke. I just couldn't believe it, we were saved. That broken bar was about the prettiest sight ever seen. We (Miller and I) called out to Lt. Ben to go first and try to get to safety. We could not have lasted another 5 minutes I am sure.

For some reason I felt that Lt. Ben is the best friend I've got and that at all cost he should go free. Now don't get me wrong, I had no ax to grind, the last time to the parole board I told I wanted no parole. I had talked to Mr. Akins and he just about assured me that I had work release in the bag. Lt. Ben can do nothing for me, but he did, I am sure saved my life and the lives of the other 9 inmates from certain and agonizing death. Therefore he was the most important person in the world to me. Miller likewise had nothing to gain but he felt as I did.

We sent out one other man then I went out, Miller stayed in and pushed while the two of us on the outside pulled him out. One got stuck and to this day is sore from the tremendous efforts we made to pull him free.

Miller beat the bars a little to the side so that another big man might get through. I think that I broke his ribs pulling on him. When we were all free I went to C block but couldn't get in so seeing sub C gate open I went down there with inmate Cornell to inmate Strubal's cell. We were both sick and lay down there until we were sent to the yard the next day.

Lt. Ben, I feel stands 10 feet tall and should be commended for his efforts, his ability to stand fast and to think well under the stress and fear of death.

Testimonial by Leonard E. Miller:

This is a summary of what went though my mind in general the evening of the riot: Eight hobby shop participants and myself, upon leaving the hobby shop Saturday night at ring in, had just been shook down by Lt. Ben. Roger Pullen and myself were in the front of the nine men and upon and upon reaching the bottom of the stairs leading into the Control Center, some unusual action caused me to hold up a second before stepping into the Control Center. Over by the door leading into the Control Center I saw a uniformed Officer on the floor and an inmate standing over him. This more or less alerted me, but I still had no idea a riot was taking place. I concluded it was an individual beef between an Officer and a con. I saw another Officer come out of the Control Center door with a short billy or what looked like a cut off ball bat. This Officer was Lt. Pribble and I believe he may have had the same idea that I had. At any rate he was going to the assistance of the Officer that was down. Then I saw other cons moving across the Control Center with various weapons in their hands, swinging in any manner and apparently at anything. I turned and told my buddy, "come on, this isn't any place for us." When we turned and headed back up the stairs, apparently the other 7 men felt the same

     THOMAS TOOMBS, PhD

way because they were on their way back up stairs also. When we reached the top of the stairs leading into the Library, we met Lt. Ben preparing to lock up. At this point, I think he could see from my expression that something was wrong because he became very alert. I suggested to him that maybe he should let us all go into the Library and he could sort of keep an eye on us. He asked me what was up and I told him that I believed there was a riot in progress and that it wasn't safe to cross the Control Center, also that none of us cared to be involved in it. By this time the rest of the men had gone into the Library. He locked the outside steel door and suggested we all sit down at the center reading table and stay out of sight of the windows. Lt. Ben then got on the telephone and tried to make contact, I don't know just what he was able to find out, but I do know that just shortly after that he tried again and the line was dead. I talked to the other men and they all agreed that we should aid Lt. Ben in whatever way was necessary to safeguard his and our own welfare. It was my opinion and also the other men's that whatever was taking place would not succeed and we all thought that control would be restored shortly. I am one of the men in here that personally did not care much for Warden Gladden's type of administration and not knowing how sick he was, I felt that a riot attempted and failed would only serve to keep him in office longer. Had I known a riot was eminent I'd have done my best to prevent it within reason. After about 30-45 minutes, the smoke was coming very bad and the Lt mentioned that it looked as though if we didn't do something for our-

selves we just might become tapped. He had scouted the windows in an attempt to evaluate the situation. I suggested to him that maybe we would be in better shape to move into the hobby shop where we had tools that could be utilized. It may seem I took liberties not proper, but I had worked for Lt. Ben for several years, first in the Clothing Room and then as his orderly when he had charge of the Library and hobby shop. He knew me well and I knew him to be an Officer that would back his men and was able to handle the responsibility. I felt that he would need cooperation in whatever move was undertaken, also I am fairly well respected by the majority of the cons and in the event of any outside interference or attempt by anyone to injure him or anyone of the group, I could make myself felt. Lt. Ben and I discussed and rejected a couple of ideas, I advanced the idea that we go back to the Chapel and obtain aid from the front end to cut the bars out of the windows. Lt. Ben vetoed that because we would be unable to get through the locked steel door in the Chapel. By this time the smoke was getting bad. My buddy and I then told Lt. Ben that we would go with him through the Control Center, but he was reluctant to do this because he didn't want to put us in bad with the rest of the cons or maybe cause us to get hurt. But finally when it looked like that was just about the only route left, I went partly down the stairs after Lt. Ben had unlocked the outside door to the corridor. It was obvious then that no one was going to get in from the outside. I was familiar with the stairs and could run them blind but after reaching the next floor (the Classification Floor), I knew If the

   THOMAS TOOMBS, PhD

bottom door was locked I'd be a dead man because I could never make it back to the top floor again. I knew also that the other men with me could not make that stairway because the smoke was solid and boiling like a stove-pipe. I went back into the hobby shop where the most of the men were holding their heads as close to the bars as possible to obtain whatever fresh air they could. Several men, myself included were approved for metal work. One other man and myself (William Brown) to our propane tanks that we use for silver soldering and attempted to draw the temper from the bars in the window so that we could cut them, but the tanks could not generate enough heat to do any good. Lt. Ben grabbed a hand saw and tried it, it was a surprise to me that the saw would touch the bars but it did. We then got another saw that was made for cutting light metal. In the meantime, some of the cons from the outside climbed on the roof between the hobby shop and the old Dining Room and gave us aid from there. They sent up a hose with water, this was done by a fellow I know by sight but not by name. There are three of us that run together in here, Roger Pullen, Cy Griffin and myself—I found out later that Cy Griffin had been to both of our cells and when he found out that we were not home, he started looking for us. He knew that Roger and I both had been in the hobby shop earlier so he headed for the roof to find out what was the matter. We told him that we needed heavy tools to work with if he couldn't get a cutting torch. He and two other cons came back with a sledge hammer. By this time Lt. Ben and I taking turns, had one *bar just about cut out. We took the hammer and knocked it the rest of the way out. We then started on the second bar which was a little harder. Lt. Ben went out first because I wanted him to make it out as quick as possible but he stayed on the roof and waited until we had all gotten out before he left. My general impression of the whole thing was that we were fortunate to have a level headed Officer with us. The men that started the ball rolling were not the least bit concerned with how many cons got hurt or anything else. They proved this by coming back later that night and setting fire to the hobby shop from inside. This act hurt no one but the cons who worked in the hobby shop and cost us, I would guess, somewhere between 15 to 20 thousand dollars. I know this is a small sum compared to the 2 million that it cost the State , but it was all we had and some of the men just starting in the hobby shop had borrowed from their savings. One man in that position who lost only $50.00 lost just as much as I did I figure I lost close to two thousand figuring my leather goods at retail. I know that I would not have sold what was in my locker for two thousand.*

At the risk of hurting myself, I can not help but say that this entire situation could have been avoided had the emphasis years ago been towards rehabilitation and constructive training rather than the vindictive punishment that was Warden Gladden's philosophy. This man is dead and much has been said by Newspapers about what a wonderful man he was. He will likely go down in history as a hero among Criminology circles. He was far from that. The prison records

    THOMAS TOOMBS, PhD

if anyone was interested in doing a little research are full of men who came to this prison 3 & 4 times losers who never had a crime of violence on them, but after doing time under Warden Gladden's administration, they went out and picked up a gun. Several of them killed and were killed. In the 14 ½ years I have been in this prison of 15 hundred men, I've seen more brutality and suicides than I saw in 7 years in San Quentin with 6000 cons. If this is the mark of a good Warden then I am a stupid man. In closing, I will say this, there have been remarkable improvements in the last three months. What is more important, there is every indication that there are more to come. The population in general is well pleased with Warden Cupp and Captain Pribble. They are both fair men. The Prison has good men in Watson, Wenger, Ben, Sullivan and many more that I'm not personally acquainted with. We all know that there must be discipline and that you cannot satisfy everyone but there should be a set of rules and regulations in every man's cell and these rules should not be added to at the whim of individual Officers. These rules should be enforced with common sense and good judgement. I have talked too much, I have a name for being frank and opinionated, but to whomever this may concern, if it is of any help, I do not regret having said any part of it.

Testimonial unsigned, author unknown:

On Saturday March 9, 1968, at approximately three fifty in the evening Lt. Ben opened the hobby shop door and started his usual shakedown of the Cons as they prepared to return to their cells. My cell partner and I stood watching the shakedown from inside the Library. A friend of ours came out of the hobby shop and into the Library waiting so we could go down together. When Lt. Ben finisher with the shakedown he checked the hobby shop and returned to the Library to get his coat and the blue bag that had legal papers and other materials inside. But before we could leave a couple of Cons from the hobby shop returned short of breath saying there was a riot going on that Cons and Officers were fighting in the Control Center. Within a minute four more members of the hobby shop returned with the same story. Lt. Ben not knowing if this was true or not proceeded to lock the outer gate and the Library door. I might say at this time Lt. Ben had nine Cons that didn't want to go down stairs no matter what. This in itself forced him to remain in the Library with the rest of us. By this time we could all hear the noise from below.

Lt. Ben called out front and sounded the alarm within two minutes of the outbreak. I believe this to have been the first alarm sounded because from what I could hear the front had no idea that anything was happening. Lt. Ben had to repeat himself a couple of times before being understood. I guess the guy out front just couldn't believe it. After a couple of minutes Lt. Ben made an attempt to call out front again but got no answer. At Lt. Ben's suggestion we all sat at some tables in the center of the Library. We could not be seen from where were, but, Lt. Ben was able to keep watch on the outer gate so that if anyone tried to get in he would have had time to stop them.

We decided unanimously to back Lt. Ben no matter how he went. We knew that no one could get in unless Lt. Ben wanted them to. Lt. Ben made another call but I have no idea what he was told.

There was a great deal of yelling and screaming coming from the blocks. Then we heard the windows in the blocks go with a crashing noise. We could just pick up pieces of what they were yelling. We were sure that everything would be over soon but it wasn't. We waited what seemed an eternity before we even heard the sirens of the approaching police. We did hear the siren of the Penitentiary at about 4:10 p.m. and again at about 4:15 p.m. for recall. I guess it was about 4:40 p.m. before we heard the first siren of the police cars arriving. It was shortly before this that we first smelled smoke, and by around 5:10 p.m. or so it became pretty thick. Lt. Ben had been watching the outside gate from inside the Bindery Room where he could see but not be seen. He came out and motioned us all to come. He opened the door to the hobby shop and we all went in there. We could then see the fires from the Paint Shop, Print Shop and Furniture Factory. We now knew that the prison belonged to the prisoners. Lt. Ben went through the smoke and into the Library again to use the phone. The smoke was so thick I could no see him, but after about a minute he reappeared. I don't know who he called, but he said we could through the Records Office on the Classification floor. We all started out holding onto each other in a chain because the smoke was so thick we couldn't see. It was no use, the smoke and heat drove us back into the hobby shop. After a short time one of the Cons and Lt. Ben tried to get into the Chapel, but to no avail. By now Lt. Ben was not worried what the Cons would do to him, he just wanted to get us all out alive, so he called to a couple of Cons outside the window of the hobby shop working a fire hose to keep the fire from spreading any further. Lt. Ben asked them to get a cutting torch. This is the first that the Cons even knew we were in there. They hollered for hacksaws and Lt. Ben told them again that we needed cutting torches. When we told the police would cut us out soon as the Cons left the area Lt Ben tried to reason with them but it was no good they were not going to leave.

One of the Cons that was with us got a wood saw and I really thought he was crazy from the smoke. The smoke was so thick you couldn't see from one window to the next. We got a hose passed in which my cell partner handled while Lt. Ben and a couple of the Cons sawed at the bars. With the aid of a sledge hammer that a Con handed up to us we were able to get the two bars out. The sledge hammer broke once but was fixed in short order. Lt. Ben was first out the window. I wasn't sure but I thought Lt. Ben had climbed off the right side of the building in a play for freedom. All nine Convicts and Lt. Ben were saved because of everyone remaining cool during a time of crisis.

Everyone was wishing there was an emergency exit, but there was none. We could have all died of suffication or burned if hadn't been for Lt. Ben's

     THOMAS TOOMBS, PhD

leadership and keeping everyone as cool and collected as possible.

Testimonial by Charles K. Thompson:

At about 4:10 or 4:15 P.M. March 9, '68 a group of us were decending the stairs from the hobby shop to the Control Center. On arriving at the door entering into the Control Center, it took only a glance to recognize that a riot was in progress and the Control had been lost. We returned to the hobby shop floor and informed Lt. Ben.

Lt. Ben locked the steel door, turned out the lights and told us to go into the Library. We sat at a table discussing the situation in modulated voices so as not to attract attention from the outside. By this time shouts and breaking of glass could be heard in "D" and "E" blocks. Some of the sounds could be taken for tear gas, Lt Ben voiced this possibility, however we smelled no gas so this supposition we knew was in error. Smoke was creeping in at this time although not in great quantity.

Lt. Ben changed locks on the steel door to confuse anyone who might have gotten keys from the Control Center and would try to get in

We gave Lt. Ben a vote of confidence and told him that we would help break as many arms and heads as we had to in order to keep any rioters from entering.

Lt. Ben and Bob Miller took up watch from the Book Binding Room on the entrance landing so that if anyone appeared they could notify us.

In time the Library became so full of smoke and gasses that we had to abandon and retire to the hobby shop which was a little better. Very soon, it too became as bad as the Library and our objective was forced to change from defending to one of evacuation.

We formed a human chain after Lt. Ben unlocked the door and tried to make it down the stairwell. This was under Lt. Ben's orders and although if we could have made it and saved our lives Lt. Ben would have been hopping from the frying pan into the fire. Several of the men close to me were not enthused about taking this route for that reason and said as much when I mentioned it. We tried this method twice but the heat, gasses and smoke were too much even with soaked clothing and soaked rags over our faces.

There were saw blades in the hobby shop and Lt. Ben made good use of them. With help from the out-side in the form of water and a sledge hammer and several men helping we all made it out O.K.

There was a little trouble when it came my turn to go out. The hole didn't fit and it took some heaving and ho-ing and a couple of cracked ribs to make it.

After Ben was O.K., we all joined the rest of the prison population in the yard.

Lt. Ben was cool and used common sense all through the operation. I have been in combat with a number of men who were not lacking in raw courage, but in a tight spot it takes a great deal more than just courage and Lt. Ben Certainly showed that he is capable of this.

Lt Ben, in my opinion, was "the unsung hero" of that horribly destructive night and never received suf-

 THOMAS TOOMBS, PhD

A Native American, Lt. Ben is a man of honor and principle who maintained respect for the sanctity of human life, no matter how loathsome some of the human beings he had to deal with might be. Lt Ben was the unsung hero of the riot. Fortunately no one, inmate or employee, died as a result of the riot. Lt Ben is responsible for saving the lives of nine inmates who would otherwise be dead

Bibliography

Agnew, R. *Pressured Into Crime: An Overview of Strain Theory.* Los Angeles: Roxbury Publishing, 2006.

Alcock, J. *Animal Behavior: An Evolutionary Approach.* 7th ed. Sunderland, CT: Sinauer Associates, Inc., 2001.

Alexander, J. C. and P. Smith. *The Cambridge Companion to Durkheim.* New York: Cambridge University Press, 2005.

Alexander, M. "Sexual Offender Treatment Efficacy Revisited." *Sexual Abuse: A Journal of Research and Treatment* 11 (2), 101–16.

American Bar Association, Justice Kennedy Commission. "Report to the House of Delegates." http://www.abanet.org/crimijust/kennedy.

American Correctional Association. "Standards & Accreditation." http://www.aca.org.standards.

American Psychiatric Association. *Diagnostic and Statistical Manual of Mental Disorders.* 4th ed. Washington, DC: American Psychiatric Association, 2010.

Anderson, D. A. "The Aggregate Burden of Crime." *Journal of Law and Economics* 42 (2): 611–42.

Anderson, J. R. *Cognitive Psychology and Its Implications.* 5th ed. New York: Worth Publishing, 1995.

Arraj, J., and T. Arraj. *William Sheldon: A Forgotten Giant of American Psychology*. Chiloquin, OR: Inner Growth Books, 1994.

Ashton, C. H. *Chemical Imbalance*. Newcastle County of Tyne and Wear: School of Neurosciences, Division of Psychiatry, 2001.

Beardsley, M. C., ed. *European Philosophers from Descartes to Nietzsche*. Toronto: Random House, 1988.

Beck, A. R. *Recidivism: A Fruit-Salad Concept in the Criminal Justice System*. http://www.justiceconcepts. com/recidivism.

Becker, H. *Outsiders: Studies in the Sociology of Deviance*. New York: Free Press, 1963.

Bedau, H. A. *The Death Penalty in America*. New York: Oxford University Press, 1982.

Bedau, H., and P. Cassel, eds. *Debating the Death Penalty: Should America Have Capital Punishment?* New York: Oxford University Press, 2004.

Bentham, J. *An Introduction to the Principles of Morals and Legislation*. New York: Oxford University Press, 1996.

Berk, R. *New Claims About Executions and General Deterrence: Déjà Vu All Over Again*. http://www.stat. ucla.edu.

Berlin, I., ed. *The Age of Enlightenment: The 18th Century Philosophers*. Boston: Houghton Mifflin, 1956.

     THOMAS TOOMBS, PhD

Bonczar, T. P., and T. L. Snell. *Capital Punishment 2004.* Washington, DC: Department of Justice 2004.

Braithwaite, J. *Crime, Shame and Reintegration.* London: Cambridge University Press, 1989.

Bufkin, J. L., and V. R. Luttrell. "Neuroimaging Studies of Aggressive and Violent Behavior: Current Implications for Criminology and Criminal Justice" in *Trauma, Violence & Abuse* 6 (2): 176–91.

Buss, D. M. *Evolutionary Psychology: the New Science of the Mind.* Boston: Allyn and Bacon, 1999.

Campling, P., and R. Haigh, eds. *Therapeutic Communities: Past, Present and Future.* London: Jessica Kingsley Publishers, 1999.

Carcach, S. L. *Recidivism Among Juvenile Offenders: An Analysis of Times to Reappearance in Court.* Australia:Australian Capital Territory Court Research and Public Policy1999.

Cassell, P. G. "In Defense of the Death Penalty" in *Debating the Death Penalty: Should America Have Capital Punishment?* H. Bedau and P. Cassel, eds. New York: Oxford University Press, 2004.

Clarke, R. G. and Mayhew, P. (eds.) (1980). "Designing out crime." Home Office and Research Planning Unit. Online: http://www.aic.gov.au/publications/ crimeprev/part3.

Classen, R. *Restorative Justice—Fundamental Principles.* Fresno, CA Center for Peacemaking and Conflict Studies, Fresno Pacific University, 1995.

Cloward, R., and L. Ohlin. *Opportunity Delinquency*. New York: Free Press, 1960.

Cohen, A. *Delinquent Boys*. Glencoe, Ill: Free Press, 1955.

Cohen, R. L. "Probation and Parole Violators in State Prison, 1991." Washington, DC: Bureau of Justice Statistics, 1995.

Corey, Gerald. *Theory and Practice of Counseling and Psychotherapy*. 4th ed. Pacific Grove, CA: Brooks/ Cole Publishing Company, 1991.

Cosmides, L., and J. Tooby, eds., and J. H. Barkow. *The Psychological Foundations of Culture in the Adapted Mind*. New York: Oxford University Press, 1992.

Crawford, A., and J. Gooley, eds. *Integrating a Victim Perspective within Criminal Justice*: International Debates. Brookfield, VT: Ashgate, 2000.

Crawford, C. B., and D. L. Krebs, eds. *Handbook of Evolutionary Psychology: Ideas, Issues, and Applications*. Mahwah, NJ: Lawrence Erlbaum, 1998.

Cronin, H. *The Ant and the Peacock: Altruism and Sexual Selection from Darwin to Today*. London: Cambridge University Press, 2003.

Currie, E. *Crime and Punishment in America*. New York: Henry Holt and Company, 1998.

Danks, H. "Judge Rejects Slave Trauma as Defense in Boy's Killing." *The Oregonian*, May 31, 2004.

Davey, J. D. *The Politics of Prison Expansion: Winning Elections by Waging War on Crime.* Westport, CT: Praeger, 1998.

DeGruy-Leary, J. *Post-Traumatic Slave Syndrome: America's Legacy of Enduring Injury and Healing.* Milwaukee, Oregon: Uptone Press, 2005.

Dezhbakhsh, H., P. H. Rubin, and J. M. Shepherd. "Does Capital Punishment Have a Deterrent Effect? New Evidence from Post-Moratorium Panel Data." *American Law and Economics Review*, 5 (2): 344–76.

De Leon, G. *The Therapeutic Community: Theory, Model and Method.* New York: Springer Publishing Company, 2000.

DiIulio, J. J. Jr., G. P. Alpert, M. H. Moore, G. F. Cole, J. Petersilia, C. H. Logan, and J. Q. Wilson. *Performance Measures for the Criminal Justice System.* Washington, DC: Department of Justice, 1993.

DSQIC Staff. "Brain Development: Foundations for Learning & Behavior." DSQIC Dispatch. Logan, UT: Head Start Region VIII, Disability Services Quality Improvement Center. 2002

Eaton, T. "There Are No Chemical Imbalances." Fores Research Center. http://www.etfrc.com.

Ehrlich, I. "The Deterrent Effect of Capital Punishment: A Question of Life and Death." *American Economic Review* 65 (3): 397–417.

Elster, J. (ed.). *Rational Choice*. Oxford: Basil Blackwell, 1986.

Farkas, M. A., and A. Stichman. "Sex Offender Laws: Can Treatment, Punishment, Incapacitation and Public Safety Be Reconciled?" *Criminal Justice Review* 27 (2): 256–83.

Federal Bureau of Investigation. "Uniform Crime Report: Crime in the United States, 2004." Washington, DC: US Department of Justice, 2005.

Fishbein, D., and S. Pease. "The Effects of Diet on Behavior: Implications for Criminology and Corrections." *Research in Corrections* 1 (2): Washington, DC: Robert J. Kutak Foundation and the National Institute of Correction, 1988.

George, R. L., and T. S. Cristiani. *Counseling Theory and Practice*. 3rd ed. Englewood Cliffs, NJ: Prentice Hall, 1990.

Gesch, C. B., S. M. Hammond, S. E. Hampson, A. Eves, and M. J. Crowder. "Influence of Supplementary Vitamins, Minerals and Essential Fatty Acids on the Antisocial Behavior of Young Adult Prisoners." *British Journal of Psychiatry* 181: 22–8.

Gest, T. *Crime and Politics: Big Government's Erratic Campaign for Law and Order*. New York: Oxford University Press, 2001.

Gibson, M. *Born to Crime: Cesare Lombroso and the Origins of Biological Criminology*. West Port, CT: Praeger, 2002.

Gillespie, R. *Manufacturing Knowledge: A History of the Hawthorne Experiments.* Cambridge: Cambridge University Press, 1991.

Gilling, D. *Theory, Policy, and Politics.* London: Taylor & Francis Ltd, 1997.

Giordano, V. "Don't Fear Theory, The Role of Criminal Theory on Your Department's Policies." *Public Safety, Relevant Insights by the Experts.* InPublicSafety.com, American Military University, July 23,2014.

Glaze, L. E., and S. Pella. "Probation and Parole in the United States, 2004." *Bureau of Justice Statistics Bulletin.* Washington, DC: U. S. Department of Justice, 2005.

Glueck, S., and E. Glueck. *Physique and Delinquency.* Boston: Houghton Mifflin, 1956.

Gould, S. J. "The Confusion Over Evolution." *New York Review of Books* July 1993 39–54.

———. "Darwinian Fundamentalism." *New York Review of Books* June 1997, 34–37.

———. *The Mismeasure of Man.* New York: W. W. Norton and Company, 1981.

Hanson, R. K., and M. T. Bussiere. "Predicting Relapse: A Meta-Analysis of Sexual Offender Recidivism." *Journal of Clinical and Consulting Psychology* 66 (2): 348–62.

Hare, R. D. *Without Conscience: the Disturbing World of Psychopaths.* New York: Guilford Publications, 1998.

Harer, M. D. "Recidivism Among Federal Prisoners
    Released in 1997." *Journal of Correctional Education*
    46 (3): 98–128.

Harlow, C. W. *Education and Correctional Populations.*
    (January 2003). Washington, D. C.: Bureau of Justice
    Statistics, U. S. Department of Justice.

Harp, G. J. *The Positivist Republic: Auguste Comte and the
    Reconstruction of American Liberalism,* 1865-1920.
    University Park, PA: Pennsylvania State University
    Press, 1995.

Harris, R. A. *Creative Problem Solving: A Step-By-Step
    Approach.* Los Angles: Pyrczak Publishing, 2002.

Herival, T., and P. Wright, eds. *Prison Nation: the
    Warehousing of America's Poor.* New York: Routledge,
    2003.

Herman, P. G. *The American Prison System.* New York: H.
    W. Wilson Publishing Company, 2001.

Hirschi, T. *Causes of Delinquency.* Berkeley and Los
    Angles: University of California Press, 1969.

Huff, C. R., A. Rattner, and E. Sagarin, eds. *Convicted But
    Innocent: Wrongful Conviction and Public Policy,*
    Thousand Oaks, CA: Sage Publication, 1996.

Hughes, K. A. *Justice Expenditures and Employment in the
    United States, 2003.* Washington, DC: United States
    Department of Justice, 2006.

Ivey, A. E., M. D'Andrea, M. Ivey, and L. Simek-Morgan. *Theories of Counseling and Psychotherapy.* 5th ed. Needham, MA: Allyn & Bacon, 2002.

Jeffery, C. R. *Crime Prevention Through Environmental Design.* Beverly Hills: Sage, 1971.

Jenkins, J. "Face Facts: A History of Physiognomy from Ancient Mesopotamia to the End of the 19th Century." *Journal of Biocommunications* 24 (3): 2–7.

Johnson, B. R., D. B. Larson, and T. C. Pitts. "Religious Programs, Institutional Adjustment, and Recidivism Among Former Inmates in Prison Fellowship Programs." *Justice Quarterly* 14 (1): 145–66.

Johnston, N. B. *Forms of Constraint: A History of Prison Architecture.* Urbana, Ill.: University of Illinois Press, 2002.

Jones, W. H. *Nature of Man: Regimen in Health, Humors, Aphorisms.* Cambridge, MA: Harvard University Press, 1931.

Judd, D. K. *Taking Sides: Clashing Views on Controversial Issues in Religion.* Gilford, CT: McGraw Hill/Duskin, 2003.

Kagen, J., N. Snidman, D. Arcus, and J. S. Reznick. *Galen's Prophecy: Temperament in Human Nature.* New York: Basic Books, 1994.

Kalat, J. W. *Introduction to Psychology.* 4th ed. Belmont, CA: Wadsworth, 2005.

Kennard, D. *An Introduction to Therapeutic Communities.* London: Jessica Kingsley Publishers, 1998.

Kretschmer, Ernst. *Physique and Character: An Investigation of the Nature of Constitution and of the Theory of Temperament.* London: Routledge & Kegan, Paul Ltd., 1949.

Langan, P. A., E. L. Schmitt, and M. R. Durose. *Recidivism of Sex Offenders Released from Prison in 1994.* Washington, DC: Department of Justice, 2003.

Langan, P. A., and D. J. Levin. *Recidivism of Prisoners Released in 1994.* Washington, DC: US Department of Justice, 2002.

Lawrence, S., D. P. Mears, G. Dubin, and J. Travis. *The Practice and Promise of Prison Programming.* Washington, DC: Urban Institute Justice Policy Center, 2002.

Laycock, G. "Scientists or Politicians: Who Has the Answer to Crime?" Inaugural Address, Opening Ceremony, Jill Dando Institute of Crime Science, University College of London. http://www.jdi.ucl.ac.uk/publications.

Leichsenring, F., and E. Leibing. "The Effectiveness of Psychodynamic Therapy and Cognitive Behavior Therapy in the Treatment of Personality Disorders: A Meta-Analysis." *American Journal of Psychiatry* 160: 1223–32.

LoBuglio, S. "Time to Reframe Politics and Practices in Correctional Education" in *Annual Review of Adult*

Learning and Literacy. Cambridge, MA: National Center for the Study of Adult Learning and Literacy, 2000.

Lyons, L., and S. Scheingold. "The Politics of Crime and Punishment. The Nature of Crime: Continuity and Change." *Criminal Justice* 1, 103–149.

MacCormick, A. H. *The Education of Adult Prisoners: Foundations of Criminal Justice*. New York: AMS Press, 1931.

Mackay, C. *Schizophrenia and Other Psychotic Disorders*. Danvers, MA: Crown Publishing Group, 1995.

MacKenzie, D. L. "Results of a Multisite Study of Boot Camp Prison." Federal Probation 58 (2): 60–66.

Marshall, M. L. *Discipline Without Stress, Punishments or Rewards: How Teachers and Parents Promote Responsibility and Learning*. Los Alamitos, CA: Piper Press, 2002.

Martin, B. *Anxiety and Neurotic Disorders*. New York, NY: Wiley, 1971.

Mathieson, T. *Prison on Trial: A Critical Assessment*. Newbury Park, CA: Sage, 1990.

Meloy, J. R. *The Psychopathic Mind: Origins, Dynamics and Treatment*. Northvale, NJ: Jason Aronson Inc., 1988.

Mendez, M. F., A. K. Chen, J. S. Shapiro, and B. L. Miller. "Acquired Sociopathy and Frontal Lobe Dementia." *Dementia and Geriatric Cognitive Disorders* 20 (2–3): 99–104.

Menninger, K. *The Crime of Punishment.* New York: Viking, 1968.

Merton, R. "Social Structure and Anomie." *American Sociological Review* 3 (Oct. 1938): 672-682. Reprinted in *On Social Structure Science, essays by Robert K. Merton,* Piotr Sztompika, (ed.). Chicago: University of Chicago Press, 1996.

Meyers, G. *William James: His Life and Thoughts.* New Haven, CT: Yale University Press, 2001.

Miller, W. (1958) "Lower-Class Structure as a Generating Milieu of Gang Delinquency." *Journal of Social Issues,* 14, 9-30.

Mocan, H. N. and Gittings, R. K. *Pardons, Executions and Homicide.* (October 2001) Online: http://www.econ. cudenver.edu/beckman/kai./pdf

Moore, David B. "Shame, Forgiveness, and Juvenile Justice." *Criminal Justice Ethics* 12 (1): 3–25.

Morris, N., and Rothman, D. J. *The Oxford History of the Prison: the Practice of Punishment in Western Society.* New York: Oxford University Press, 1998.

Morse, Stephen J. "Bad or Mad? Sex Offenders and Social Control" in *Protecting Society from Sexually Dangerous Offenders: Law, Justice and Therapy.* Washington, DC: American Psychological Association, 2003.

Mumola, C. J. *Substance Abuse Treatment of State and Federal Prisoners.* Washington, DC: Department of Justice, 1999.

Oregon State Constitution, Article 1, Section 41.

Parent, D. G. *Correctional Boot Camps: Lessons from a Decade of Research*. Washington, DC: National Institute of Justice, 2003.

Parker, K. F., M. A. DeWees, and M. L. Radelet. "Race, the Death Penalty, and Wrongful Convictions." *American Bar Association Criminal Justice* 18 (1): 48–54.

Pelissier, B., S. Wallace, J. A. O'Neil, G. G. Gaes, S. Camp, W. Rhodes, and W. Saylor. "Federal Bureau of Prisons Residential Drug Treatment Reduces Substance Use and Arrest After Release." *Journal of Drug and Alcohol Abuse* 27 (2): 315–37.

Pojman, L. P. "Why the Death Penalty Is Morally Permissible" in *Debating the Death Penalty: Should America Have Capital Punishment?* New York: Oxford University Press, 2004.

President's Commission on Law Enforcement and Administration of Justice, *Challenge of Crime in a Free Society*. Washington, DC: Department of Justice, 1967.

Proussaint, A. F., and A. Alexander. *Lay My Burden Down: Unraveling Suicide and the Mental Health Crisis Among African-Americans*. Boston: Beacon Press, 2000.

Radelet, M. L., H. Hugo, A. Bedau, and C. Putnam. *In Spite of Innocence: Erroneous Convictions in Capital Cases*. Boston, MA: Northeastern University Press, 1992.

Raine, A., T. Loncz, S. Bihrle, L. LaCasse, and P. Colletti. "Reduced Prefrontal Gray Matter Volume and Reduced Autonomic Activity in Antisocial Behavior." *Archives of General Psychiatry* 57: 119–27.

Reid, O. G., S. Mims, and L. Higginbottom. *Post-Traumatic Slavery Disorder: Definition, Diagnosis and Treatment.* http://www.pyramidbuilders.org.

Rhee, S. H. and I. Waldman. "Genetic and Environmental Influences on Antisocial Behavior: A Meta-Analysis of Twin and Adoption Studies." *Psychological Bulletin* 128 (3): 490–529.

Rice, M. E., and T. H. Grant. "What We Know and Don't Know About Treating Sex Offenders" in *Protecting Society from Sexually Dangerous Offenders: Law, Justice and Therapy.* Washington, DC: American Psychological Association, 2003.

Robinson, M. B. *Why Crime? An Integrated Systems Theory of Antisocial Behavior.* Upper Saddle River, NJ: Prentice Hall, 2004.

Sabbatini, R. M. E. *Phrenology: the History of Brain Localization.* State University of Campinas. http://www.epub.org.

Samenow, S. E. *Straight Talk About Criminals: Understanding and Treating Antisocials.* Northvale, NJ: Jason Aronson Publishers, 2002.

Scott, J., G. Browning, A. Halcli, N. Hewlett, and F. Webster, eds. "Rational Choice Theory."

Understanding Contemporary Society: Theories of the Present. London: Sage, 1999.

Sherman, L. W., D. Gottfredson, D, MacKenzie, J. Eck, P. Reuter, and S. Bushway in collaboration with members of the University of Maryland Graduate Program in Criminology and Criminal Justice. *Preventing Crime: What Works, What Doesn't, What's Promising.* Washington, DC: National Institute of Justice, 1996.

Smith Prangle, L. "Moral and Criminal Responsibilities in Plato's Laws." *American Political Science Review* 103, no. 3 (2009).

Skinner, B. F. *The Behavior of Organisms: An Experimental Analysis.* Acton, MA: Copley Publishing Group, 1999.

Sutherland, E. H. *White Collar Crime.* New York: Holt, Rinehart and Winston, 1949.

Symons, D. "On the Use and Misuse of Darwinism in the Study of Human Behavior" in *The Adapted Mind: Evolutionary Psychology and the Generation of Culture.* New York: Oxford University Press, 1992.

Tannenbaum, F. *Crime and the Community.* New York: Columbia University Press, 1938.

Thompson, K., ed. *Auguste Comte: the Foundation of Sociology.* New York: Wiley & Sons, 1976.

Thorndike, E. L. *Animal Intelligence: Experimental Studies.* 2nd ed. New Brunswick, NJ: Transaction Publishers, 2000.

Thornhill, R., and C. T. Palmer. *A Natural History of Rape: Biological Bases of Sexual Coercion*. Cambridge, MA: MIT Press, 2000.

Toombs, T. G. "Monitoring and Controlling Criminal Offenders Using the Satellite Global Positioning System Coupled to Surgically Implanted Transponders: Is It a Viable Alternative to Prison?" *Criminal Justice Policy Review* 7 (3–4/95): 341–46.

United States Bureau of Justice Statistics, *Sourcebook of Criminal Justice Statistics 2003*. Washington, DC: US Department of Justice, 2005.

United States Office for the Protection from Research Risks, Institutes of Health, Department of Health and Human Services. *Title 45, Code of Federal Regulations, Part 46, Protection of Human Subjects*. August 2001.

Van Wyne, J. "The History of Phrenology on the Web." http://www.britishlibrary.net/phrenology/overview.

Walsh, W. J. "Chemical Imbalances and Criminal Violence." *NOHA News* 13 (2): 3–4.

Walsh, W. J. "Biochemistry and Behavior." *NOHA News* 19 (1): 3–4.

Walters, J. P. *Drug Treatment in the Criminal Justice System*. Washington, DC: Office of the President Office of National Drug Control Policy, 2001.

Westervelt, S., and J. Humphrey, eds. *Wrongly Convicted: Perspectives on Failed Justice*. Piscataway, NJ: Rutgers University Press, 2001.

Wilbanks, W. *The Myth of a Racist Criminal Justice System.* Monterey, CA: Brooks Cole, 1987.

Wilson, D. B., C. A., Gallagher, and D. L. McKenzie. "A Meta-Analysis of Corrections-Based Education, Vocation, and Work Programs for Adult Offenders." *Journal of Research in Crime and Delinquency* 37 (4): 347–68.

Wilson, E. O. *On Human Nature.* Cambridge, MA: Harvard University Press, 1978.

———. *Consilience: the Unity of Knowledge.* New York: Vintage Books, 1999.

Wilson, E. O. "Introduction: What Is Sociobiology?" in *Sociobiology and Human Nature: An Interdisciplinary Critique and Defense.* San Francisco: Jossey-Bass, 1978.

Wilson, J. Q. *Thinking About Crime.* New York: Random House, 1975.

Wilson, J. Q., and R. Herrnstein. *The Definitive Study of the Causes of Crime.* New York: Simon and Schuster, 1985.

Winick, B. J., and J. Q. La Fond, eds. *Protecting Society from Sexually Dangerous Offenders: Law, Justice and Therapy.* Washington, DC: American Psychological Association, 2003.

Wolfgard, M. and Ferracuti, F. *Subculture of Violence: Towards an Integrated Theory of Criminology.* New York, NY: Barnes & Noble, 1967.

Wright, R. A. *In Defense of Prisons*. Westport, CT: Greenwood Press, 1994.

Yochelson, S., and S. E. Samenow. *Criminal Personality: A Profile for Change*. Vol. 1. Northvale, NJ: Jason Aronson Publishers, 1994.

———. *The Criminal Personality: the Change Process*. Vol. 2. Northvale, NJ: Jason Aronson Publishers, 1995.

 THOMAS TOOMBS, PhD

Index

     THOMAS TOOMBS, PhD

 THOMAS TOOMBS, PhD

 THOMAS TOOMBS, PhD

     THOMAS TOOMBS, PhD

    THOMAS TOOMBS, PhD

Trump, Donald, 92

US Bureau of Justice Statistics, 9, 10, 60, 62–63, 73, 76
US Criminal Justice Information Division, 83
US Department of Education, 77
US Department of Justice, 20–21
US Food and Drug Administration, 95

Van Wyhe, J., 38
Verichip, 95
vocational training, 76–78
Voltaire, 6

Westervelt, S., 20
Wilbanks, W., 21
Wilson, D. B., 78, 81
Wilson, Edward O., 45–46, 53–54
Winick, B. J., 75
Wolfgang, 24
work camps, 15
work rehabilitation programs, 79–83

Yochelson, Samuel, 33–34, 35
Yoder, Grant, 100

www.ingramcontent.com/pod-product-compliance
Lightning Source LLC
Chambersburg PA
CBHW051451050726
47593CB00005B/2027